THE

BHĂGVĂT-GĒĒTĀ,

OR

DIALOGUES

OF

KRĔĔSHNĂ AND *ĂRJŎŎN;*

IN EIGHTEEN LECTURES;

WITH

NOTES.

TRANSLATED FROM THE ORIGINAL, IN THE *Sanſkreet*, OR ANCIENT
LANGUAGE OF THE *Brahmans*,

BY

CHARLES WILKINS,

SENIOR MERCHANT IN THE SERVICE OF THE HONOURABLE THE EAST INDIA
COMPANY, ON THEIR BENGAL ESTABLISHMENT.

LONDON:

PRINTED FOR C. NOURSE,
OPPOSITE CATHARINE-STREET, IN THE STRAND.

M.DCC.LXXXV.

MAY 30th, 1785.

ADVERTISEMENT.

THE following Work is publiſhed under the authority of the Court of Directors of the Eaſt India Company, by the particular deſire and recommendation of the Governor General of India; whoſe letter to the Chairman of the Company will ſufficiently explain the motives for its publication, and furniſh the beſt teſtimony of the fidelity, accuracy, and merit of the Tranſlator.

The antiquity of the original, and the veneration in which it hath been held for ſo many ages, by a very conſiderable portion of the human race, muſt render it one of the greateſt curioſities ever preſented to the literary world.

TO

T O

NATHANIEL SMITH, Efquire.

S I R,

TO you, as to the firft member of the first commercial body, not only of the prefent age, but of all the known generations of mankind, I prefume to offer, and to recommend through you, for an offering to the public, a very curious fpecimen of the Literature, the Mythology, and Morality of the ancient Hindoos. It is an epifodical extract from the "Mahabharat," a moft voluminous poem, affirmed to have been written upwards of four thoufand years ago, by Kreefhna Dwypayen Veiâs, a learned Bramin ; to whom is alfo attributed the compilation of "The Four "Vêdes, or Bêdes," the only exifting original fcriptures of the religion of Brahmâ; and the compofition of all the Poorâns, which are to this day taught in their fchools, and venerated as poems of divine infpiration. Among thefe, and of fuperior eftimation to the reft, is ranked the Mahabharat. But if the feveral books here enumerated be really the productions of their reputed author, which is greatly to be doubted, many arguments may be adduced to afcribe to the fame fource the invention of the religion itfelf, as well as its promulgation: and he muft, at all events, claim the merit of having firft reduced the grofs and fcattered tenets of their former faith into a fcientific and allegorical fyftem.

The Mahabharat contains the genealogy and general hiftory of the houfe of Bhaurut, fo called from Bhurrut, its founder; the epithet Mahâ, or Great, being prefixed in token of diftinction: but

its

its more particular object is to relate the diffentions and wars of the two great collateral branches of it, called Kooroos and Pandoos; both lineally defcended in the fecond degree from Veecheetraveerya, their common anceftor, by their refpective fathers Dreetrarafhtra and Pandoo.

The Kooroos, which indeed is fometimes ufed as a term comprehending the whole family, but moft frequently applied as the patronymic of the elder branch alone, are faid to have been one hundred in number, of whom Dooryodun was efteemed the head and reprefentative even during the life of his father, who was incapacitated by blindnefs. The fons of Pandoo were five; Yoodhifhteer, Bheem, Arjoon, Nekool, and Sehadeo; who, through the artifices of Dooryodun, were banifhed, by their uncle and guardian Dreetrarafhtra, from Haftenapoor, at that time the feat of government of Hindoftan.

The exiles, after a feries of adventures, worked up with a wonderful fertility of genius and pomp of language into a thoufand fublime defcriptions, returned with a powerful army to avenge their wrongs, and affert their pretenfions to the empire in right of their father; by whom, though the younger brother, it had been held while he lived, on account of the difqualification already mentioned of Dreetrarafhtra.

In this ftate the epifode opens, and is called "The Geeta of "Bhagvat," which is one of the names of Kreefhna. Arjoon is reprefented as the favorite and pupil of Kreefhna, here taken for God himfelf, in his laft Ootâr, or defcent to earth in a mortal form.

The Preface of the Tranflator will render any further explanation of the Work unneceffary. Yet fomething it may be allowable for me to add refpecting my own judgment of a Work which I have thus informally obtruded on your attention, as it is the only ground on which I can defend the liberty which I have taken.

Might I, an unlettered man, venture to prefcribe bounds to the latitude of criticifm, I fhould exclude, in eftimating the merit of fuch a production, all rules drawn from the ancient or modern literature of Europe, all references to fuch fentiments or manners as are become the ftandards of propriety for opinion and action in our own modes of life, and equally all appeals to our revealed tenets of religion and moral duty. I fhould exclude them, as by no means applicable to the language, fentiments, manners, or morality

rality appertaining to a fyftem of fociety with which we have been for ages unconnected, and of an antiquity preceding even the firft efforts of civilization in our own quarter of the globe, which, in refpect to the general diffufion and common participation of arts and fciences, may be now confidered as one community.

I would exact from every reader the allowance of obfcurity, abfurdity, barbarous habits, and a perverted morality. Where the reverfe appears, I would have him receive it (to ufe a familiar phrafe) as so much clear gain, and allow it a merit proportioned to the difappointment of a different expectation.

In effect, without befpeaking this kind of indulgence, I could hardly venture to perfift in my recommendation of this production for public notice.

Many paffages will be found obfcure, many will feem redundant; others will be found cloathed with ornaments of fancy unfuited to our tafte, and fome elevated to a track of fublimity into which our habits of judgment will find it difficult to purfue them; but few which will fhock either our religious faith or moral fentiments. Something too muft be allowed to the fubject itfelf, which is highly metaphyfical, to the extreme difficulty of rendering abftract terms by others exactly correfponding with them in another language, to the arbitrary combination of ideas, in words expreffing unfubftantial qualities, and more, to the errors of interpretation. The modefty of the Tranflator would induce him to defend the credit of his work, by laying all its apparent defects to his own charge, under the article laft enumerated; but neither does his accuracy merit, nor the work itfelf require that conceffion.

It is alfo to be obferved, in illuftration of what I have premifed, that the Brahmans are enjoined to perform a kind of fpiritual difcipline, not, I believe, unknown to fome of the religious orders of Chriftians in the Romifh Church. This confifts in devoting a certain period of time to the contemplation of the Deity, his attributes, and the moral duties of this life. It is required of thofe who practife this exercife, not only that they diveft their minds of all fenfual defire, but that their attention be abftracted from every external object, and abforbed, with every fenfe, in the prefcribed fubject of their meditation. I myfelf was once a witnefs of a man employed in this fpecies of devotion, at the principal temple of Banaris. His right hand and arm were enclofed in a loofe fleeve or bag of red cloth, within which he paffed the beads of his ro-

fary,

fary, one after another, through his fingers, repeating with the touch of each (as I was informed) one of the names of God, while his mind laboured to catch and dwell on the idea of the quality which appertained to it, and shewed the violence of its exertion to attain this purpose by the convulsive movements of all his features, his eyes being at the same time closed, doubtless to assist the abstraction. The importance of this duty cannot be better illustrated, nor stronger marked, than by the last sentence with which Kreeshna closes his instruction to Arjoon, and which is properly the conclusion of the Geeta: "Hath what I have been "speaking, O Arjoon, been heard *with thy mind fixed to one point?* "Is the *distraction* of thought, which arose from thy ignorance, re- "moved?"

To those who have never been accustomed to this separation of the mind from the notices of the senses, it may not be easy to conceive by what means such a power is to be attained; since even the most studious men of our hemisphere will find it difficult so to restrain their attention but that it will wander to some object of present sense or recollection; and even the buzzing of a fly will sometimes have the power to disturb it. But if we are told that there have been men who were successively, for ages past, in the daily habit of abstracted contemplation, begun in the earliest period of youth, and continued in many to the maturity of age, each adding some portion of knowledge to the store accumulated by his predecessors; it is not assuming too much to conclude, that, as the mind ever gathers strength, like the body, by exercise, so in such an exercise it may in each have acquired the faculty to which they aspired, and that their collective studies may have led them to the discovery of new tracks and combinations of sentiment, totally different from the doctrines with which the learned of other nations are acquainted: doctrines, which however speculative and subtle, still, as they possess the advantage of being derived from a source so free from every adventitious mixture, may be equally founded in truth with the most simple of our own. But as they must differ, yet more than the most abstruse of ours, from the common modes of thinking, so they will require consonant modes of expression, which it may be impossible to render by any of the known terms of science in our language, or even to make them intelligible by definition. This is probably the case with some of the English phrases, as those of "Action," "Application," "Practice," &c. which occur in

Mr.

Mr. Wilkins's tranflation ; and others, for the reafons which I have recited, he has left with the fame founds in which he found them. When the text is rendered obfcure from fuch caufes, candor requires that credit be given to it for fome accurate meaning, though we may not be able to difcover it ; and that we afcribe their obfcurity to the incompetency of our own perceptions, on fo novel an appli-- cation of them, rather than to the lefs probable want of perfpicuity in the original compofition.

With the deduftions, or rather qualifications, which I have thus premifed, I hefitate not to pronounce the Geeta a performance of great originality; of a fublimity of conception, reafoning, and diction, almoft unequalled ; and a fingle exception, among all the known religions of mankind, of a theology accurately correfponding with that of the Chriftian difpenfation, and moft powerfully illuftrating its fundamental doftrines.

It will not be fair to try its relative worth by a comparifon with the original text of the firft ftandards of European compofition ; but let thefe be taken even in the moft efteemed of their profe tranflations ; and in that equal fcale let their merits be weighed. I fhould not fear to place, in oppofition to the beft French verfions of the moft admired paffages of the Iliad or Odyffey, or of the 1ft and 6th Books of our own Milton, highly as I venerate the latter, the Englifh tranflation of the Mahabharat.

One blemifh will be found in it, which will fcarcely fail to make its own impreffion on every correft mind ; and which for that reafon I anticipate. I mean, the attempt to defcribe fpiritual exiftences by terms and images which appertain to corporeal forms. Yet even in this refpeft it will appear lefs faulty than other works with which I have placed it in competition; and, defeftive as it may at firft appear, I know not whether a doftrine fo elevated above common perception did not require to be introduced by fuch ideas as were familiar to the mind, to lead it by a gradual advance to the pure and abftraft comprehenfion of the fubjeft. This will feem to have been, whether intentionally or accidentally, the order which is followed by the author of the Geeta ; and fo far at leaft he foars far beyond all competitors in this fpecies of compofition. Even the frequent recurrence of the fame fentiment, in a variety of drefs, may have been owing to the fame confideration of the extreme intricacy of the fubjeft, and the confequent neceffity of trying different kinds of exemplification and argument, to imprefs it with due

2   conviction

conviction on the underftanding. Yet I believe it will appear, to an attentive reader, neither deficient in method, nor in perfpicuity. On the contrary, I thought it at the firft reading, and more fo at the fecond, clear beyond what I could have reafonably expected, in a difcuffion of points fo far removed beyond the reach of the fenfes, and explained through fo foreign a medium.

It now remains to fay fomething of the Tranflator, Mr. Charles Wilkins. This Gentleman, to whofe ingenuity, unaided by models for imitation, and by artifts for his direction, your government is indebted for its printing-office, and for many official purpofes to which it has been profitably applied, with an extent unknown in Europe, has united to an early and fuccefsful attainment of the Perfian and Bengal languages, the ftudy of the Sanfkreet. To this he devoted himfelf with a perfeverance of which there are few examples, and with a fuccefs which encouraged him to undertake the tranflation of the Mahabharat. This book is faid to confift of more than one hundred thoufand metrical ftanzas, of which he has at this time tranflated more than a third ; and, if I may truft to the imperfect tefts by which I myfelf have tried a very fmall portion of it, through the medium of another language, he has rendered it with great accuracy and fidelity. Of its elegance, and the fkill with which he has familiarized (if I may fo exprefs it) his own native language to fo foreign an original, I may not fpeak, as from the fpecimen herewith prefented, whoever reads it, will judge for himfelf.

Mr. Wilkins's health having fuffered a decline from the fatigues of bufinefs, from which his gratuitous labors allowed him no relaxation, he was advifed to try a change of air for his recovery. I myfelf recommended that of Banaris, for the fake of the additional advantage which he might derive from a refidence in a place which is confidered as the firft feminary of Hindoo learning ; and I promoted his application to the Board, for their permiffion to repair thither, without forfeiting his official appointments during the term of his abfence.

I have always regarded the encouragement of every fpecies of ufeful diligence, in the fervants of the Company, as a duty appertaining to my office ; and have feverely regretted that I have poffeffed fuch fcanty means of exercifing it, efpecially to fuch as required an exemption from official attendance ; there being few emoluments in
this

this fervice but fuch as are annexed to official employment, and few offices without employment. Yet I believe I may take it upon me to pronounce, that the fervice has at no period more abounded with men of cultivated talents, of capacity for bufinefs, and liberal knowledge; qualities which reflect the greater luftre on their pof-feffors by having been the fruit of long and laboured application, at a feafon of life, and with a licence of conduct, more apt to produce diffipation than excite the defire of improvement.

Such ftudies, independently of their utility, tend, efpecially when the purfuit of them is general, to diffufe a generofity of fentiment, and a difdain of the meaner occupations of fuch minds as are left nearer to the ftate of uncultivated nature; and you, Sir, will be-lieve me, when I affure you, that it is on the virtue, not the ability of their fervants, that the Company muft rely for the permanency of their dominion.

Nor is the cultivation of language and fcience, for fuch are the ftudies to which I allude, ufeful only in forming the moral charac-ter and habits of the fervice. Every accumulation of knowledge, and efpecially fuch as is obtained by focial communication with people over whom we exercife a dominion founded on the right of conqueft, is ufeful to the ftate: it is the gain of humanity: in the fpecific inftance which I have ftated, it attracts and conciliates dif-tant affections; it leffens the weight of the chain by which the na-tives are held in fubjection; and it imprints on the hearts of our own countrymen the fenfe and obligation of benevolence. Even in England, this effect of it is greatly wanting. It is not very long fince the inhabitants of India were confidered by many, as creatures fcarce elevated above the degree of favage life; nor, I fear, is that prejudice yet wholly eradicated, though furely abated. Every in-ftance which brings their real character home to obfervation will imprefs us with a more generous fenfe of feeling for their natural rights, and teach us to eftimate them by the meafure of our own. But fuch inftances can only be obtained in their writings: and thefe will furvive when the Britifh dominion in India fhall have long ceafed to exift, and when the fources which it once yielded of wealth and power are loft to remembrance.

If you, Sir, on the perufal of Mr. Wilkins's performance, fhall judge it worthy of fo honorable a patronage, may I take the fur-ther liberty to requeft that you will be pleafed to prefent it to the Court of Directors, for publication by their authority, and to ufe

your

your intereft to obtain it ? Its public reception will be the teft of its real merit, and determine Mr. Wilkins in the profecution or ceffation of his prefent laborious ftudies. It may, in the firft event, clear the way to a wide and unexplored field of fruitful knowledge ; and fuggeft, to the generofity of his honorable employers, a defire to encourage the firft perfevering adventurer in a fervice in which his example will have few followers, and moft probably none, if it is to be performed with the gratuitous labor of years loft to the provifion of future fubfiftence: for the ftudy of the Sanfkreet cannot, like the Perfian language, be applied to official profit, and improved with the official exercife of it. It can only derive its reward, beyond the breath of fame, in a fixed endowment. Such has been the fate of his predeceffor, Mr. Halhed, whofe labors and incomparable genius, in two ufeful productions, have been crowned with every fuccefs that the public eftimation could give them ; nor will it detract from the no lefs original merit of Mr. Wilkins, that I afcribe to another the title of having led the way, when I add, that this example held out to him no incitement to emulate it, but the profpect of barren applaufe. To fay more, would be difrefpect ; and I believe that I addrefs myfelf to a gentleman who poffeffes talents congenial with thofe which I am fo anxious to encourage, and a mind too liberal to confine its beneficence to fuch arts alone as contribute to the immediate and fubftantial advantages of the ftate.

I think it proper to affure you, that the fubject of this addrefs, and its defign, were equally unknown to the perfon who is the object of it ; from whom I originally obtained the tranflation for another purpofe, which on a fecond revifal of the work I changed, from a belief that it merited a better deftination.

A mind rendered fufceptible by the daily experience of unmerited reproach, may be excufed if it anticipates even unreafonable or improbable objections. This muft be my plea for any apparent futility in the following obfervation. I have feen an extract from a foreign work of great literary credit, in which my name is mentioned, with very undeferved applaufe, for an attempt to introduce the knowledge of Hindoo literature into the European world, by forcing or corrupting the religious confciences of the Pundits, or profeffors of their facred doctrines. This reflection was produced by the publication of Mr. Halhed's tranflation of the Poottee, or code of Hindoo laws ; and is totally devoid of foundation. For myfelf

I

I can declare truly, that if the acquisition could not have been obtained but by such means as have been supposed, I should never have sought it. It was contributed both cheerfully and gratuitously, by men of the most respectable characters for sanctity and learning in Bengal, who refused to accept more than the moderate daily subsistence of one rupee each, during the term that they were employed on the compilation; nor will it much redound to my credit, when I add, that they have yet received no other reward for their meritorious labors. Very natural causes may be ascribed for their reluctance to communicate the mysteries of their learning to strangers, as those to whom they have been for some centuries in subjection, never enquired into them, but to turn their religion into derision, or deduce from them arguments to support the intolerant principles of their own. From our nation they have received a different treatment, and are no less eager to impart their knowledge than we are to receive it. I could say much more in proof of this fact, but that it might look too much like self-commendation.

I have the honor to be, with respect,

S I R,

Your most obedient, and

Most humble Servant,

WARREN HASTINGS.

Calcutta, 3d Decr 1784.

P. S. Since the above was written, Mr. Wilkins has transmitted to me a corrected copy of his Translation, with the Preface and Notes much enlarged and improved. In the former, I meet with some complimentary passages, which are certainly improper for a work published at my own solicitation. But he is at too great a distance to allow of their being sent back to him for correction, without losing the opportunity, which I am unwilling to lose, of the present dispatch; nor could they be omitted, if I thought myself at liberty to expunge them, without requiring considerable alterations in the context. They must therefore stand; and I hope that this explanation will be admitted as a valid excuse for me in passing them.

W. H.

THE

THE

BHĂGVĂT-GĒĒTĀ,

OR

DIALOGUES

OF

KRĔĔSHNĂ AND *ĂRJŎŎN.*

TO THE HONORABLE

WARREN HASTINGS, Esq.

GOVERNOR GENERAL, &c. &c.

HONORABLE SIR,

UNCONSCIOUS of the liberal purpofe for which you intended the *Geeta*, when, at your requeft, I had the honor to prefent you with a copy of the manufcript, I was the lefs folicitous about its imperfections, becaufe I knew that your extenfive acquaintance with the cuftoms and religious tenets of the Hindoos would elucidate every paffage that was obfcure, and I had fo often experienced approbation from your partiality, and correction from your pen : It was the theme of a pupil to his preceptor and patron. But fince I received your commands to prepare it for the public view, I feel all that anxiety which muft be infeparable from one who, for the firft time, is about to appear before that awful tribunal; and I fhould dread the event, were I not convinced that the liberal fentiments expreffed in the letter you have done me the honor to write, in recommendation of the work, to the Chairman of the Direction, if permitted to accompany it to the prefs, would fcreen me, under its own intrinfic merit, from all cenfure.

3   The

The world, Sir, is fo well acquainted with your boundlefs patronage in general, and of the perfonal encouragement you have conftantly given to my fellow-fervants in particular, to render themfelves more capable of performing their duty in the various branches of commerce, revenue, and policy, by the ftudy of the languages, with the laws and cuftoms of the natives, that it muft deem the firft fruit of every genius you have raifed a tribute juftly due to the fource from which it fprang. As that perfonal encouragement alone firft excited emulation in my breaft, and urged me to profecute my particular ftudies, even beyond the line of pecuniary reward, I humbly requeft you will permit me, in token of my gratitude, to lay the *Geeta* publicly at your feet.

I have the honor to fubfcribe myfelf, with great refpect,

Honorable Sir,

Your moft obedient, and

Moft humble Servant,

Banaris,
19th November, 1784.

CHAS WILKINS.

THE

THE

TRANSLATOR's PREFACE.

THE following work, forming part of the *Mahabharat*, an ancient Hindoo poem, is a dialogue fuppofed to have paffed between *Kreefhna*, an incarnation of the Deity, and his pupil and favorite *Arjoon*, one of the five fons of *Pandoo*, who is faid to have reigned about five thoufand years ago, juft before the commencement of a famous battle fought on the plains of *Kooroo-kfhetra*, near *Dehly*, at the beginning of the *Kalee-Yoog*, or fourth and prefent age of the world, for the empire of *Bharat-verfh*, which, at that time, included all the countries that, in the prefent divifion of the globe, are called *India*, extending from the borders of *Perfia* to the extremity of *China*; and from the fnowy mountains to the fouthern promontory.

The *Brahmans* efteem this work to contain all the grand myfteries of their religion; and fo careful are they to conceal it from the knowledge of thofe of a different perfuafion, and even the vulgar of their own, that the Tranflator might have fought in vain for affiftance, had not the liberal treatment they have of late years experienced from the mildnefs of our government, the tolerating principles of our faith, and, above all, the perfonal attention paid to the learned men of their order by him under whofe aufpicious adminiftration they have fo long enjoyed, in the midft of furrounding troubles, the bleffings of internal peace, and his exemplary encouragement, at length happily created in their breafts a confidence in his countrymen fufficient to remove almoft every jealous prejudice from their minds.

It feems as if the principal defign of thefe dialogues was to unite all the prevailing modes of worfhip of thofe days; and, by fetting up the doctrine of the unity of the Godhead, in oppofition to idola-

trous

trous facrifices, and the worfhip of images, to undermine the tenets inculcated by the *Veds*; for although the author dared not
make a direct attack, either upon the prevailing prejudices of the
people, or the divine authority of thofe ancient books; yet, by offering eternal happinefs to fuch as worfhip *Brahm*, the Almighty,
whilft he declares the reward of fuch as follow other Gods fhall
be but a temporary enjoyment of an inferior heaven, for a period
meafured by the extent of their virtues, his defign was to bring
about the downfall of Polytheifm; or, at leaft, to induce men to
believe *God* prefent in every image before which they bent, and
the object of all their ceremonies and facrifices.

The moft learned *Brahmans* of the prefent times are Unitarians
according to the doctrines of *Kreefhna*; but, at the fame time that
they believe but in one God, an univerfal fpirit, they fo far comply
with the prejudices of the vulgar, as outwardly to perform all the
ceremonies inculcated by the *Veds*, fuch as facrifices, ablutions,
&c. They do this, probably, more for the fupport of their own
confequence, which could only arife from the great ignorance of
the people, than in compliance with the dictates of *Kreefhna*:
indeed, this ignorance, and thefe ceremonies, are as much the bread
of the *Brahmans*, as the fuperftition of the vulgar is the fupport of
the priefthood in many other countries.

The reader will have the liberality to excufe the obfcurity of
many paffages, and the confufion of fentiments which runs through
the whole, in its prefent form. It was the Tranflator's bufinefs to
remove as much of this obfcurity and confufion as his knowledge
and abilities would permit. This he hath attempted in his Notes;
but as he is confcious they are ftill infufficient to remove the veil
of myftery, he begs leave to remark, in his own juftification, that
the text is but imperfectly underftood by the moft learned *Brahmans* of the prefent times; and that, fmall as the work may appear, it has had more comments than the Revelations. Thefe have
not been totally difregarded; but, as they were frequently found
more obfcure than the original they were intended to elucidate, it
was thought better to leave many of the moft difficult paffages for the
exercife of the reader's own judgment, than to miflead him by fuch
wild opinions as no one fyllable of the text could authorize.

Some apology is alfo due for a few original words and proper
names that are left untranflated and unexplained. The Tranflator
was frequently too diffident of his own abilities to hazard a term
that

that did but nearly approach the fenfe of the original, and too ignorant, at prefent, of the mythology of this ancient people, to venture any very particular account, in his Notes, of fuch Deities, Saints, and Heroes, whofe names are but barely mentioned in the text. But fhould the fame Genius, whofe approbation firft kindled emulation in his breaft, and who alone hath urged him to undertake, and fupported him through the execution of far more laborious tafks than this, find no caufe to withdraw his countenance, the Tranflator may be encouraged to profecute the ftudy of the theology and mythology of the *Hindoos*, for the future entertainment of the curious.

It is worthy to be noted, that *Kreefhna*, throughout the whole, mentions only three of the four books of the *Veds*, the moft ancient fcriptures of the *Hindoos*, and thofe the firft three, according to the prefent order. This is a very curious circumftance, as it is the prefent belief that the whole four were promulgated by *Brahma* at the creation. The proof then of there having been but three before his time, is more than prefumptive, and that fo many actually exifted before his appearance ; and as the fourth mentions the name of *Kreefhna*, it is equally proved that it is a pofterior work. This obfervation has efcaped all the commentators, and was received with great aftonifhment by the *Pandeet* who was confulted in the tranflation.

The Tranflator has not as yet had leifure to read any part of thofe ancient fcriptures. He is told, that a very few of the original number of chapters are now to be found, and that the ftudy of thefe is fo difficult, that there are but few men in *Banaris* who underftand any part of them. If we may believe the *Mahabharat*, they were almoft loft five thoufand years ago ; when *Vyas*, fo named from having fuperintended the compilation of them, collected the fcattered leaves, and, by the affiftance of his difciples, collated and preferved them in four books.

THE

BHĂGVĂT-GĒĒTĀ,

OR

DIALOGUES

OF

KRĔĔSHNĂ AND *ĂRJŎŎN*.

LECTURE I.

THE GRIEF OF ARJOON.

DHREETARASHTRA *said,*

"TELL me, O *Sanjay*, what the people of my own party, and thofe of the *Pandoos*, who are affembled at *Kooroo-kfhetra* refolved for war, have been doing.

SANJAY *replied,*

" *Dooryodhan* having feen the army of the *Pandoos* drawn up for battle, went to his Preceptor, and addreffed him in the following words:"

" Behold! O mafter, faid he, the mighty army of the fons of *Pandoo* drawn forth by thy pupil, the experienced

enced fon of *Droopad.* In it are heroes, fuch as *Bheem* or *Arjoon :* there is *Yooyoodhana,* and *Veerat,* and *Droopad,* and *Dhreefhtaketoo,* and *Chekeetana,* and the valiant prince of *Kafee,* and *Pooroojeet,* and *Koonteebhoja,* and *Sivya* a mighty chief, and *Yoodhamanyoo-Veekranta,* and the daring *Ootamowja;* fo the fon of *Soobhadra,* and the fons of *Kreefhna,* the daughter of *Droopad,* all of them great in arms. Be acquainted alfo with the names of thofe of our party who are the moft diftinguifhed. I will mention a few of thofe who are amongft my generals, by way of example. There is thyfelf, my Preceptor, and *Bheefhma,* and *Kreepa* the conqueror in battle, and *Afwatthama,* and *Veekarna,* and the fon of *Sama-datta,* with others in vaft numbers who for my fervice have forfaken the love of life. They are all of them practifed in the ufe of arms, and experienced in every mode of fight. Our innumerable forces are commanded by *Bheefhma,* and the inconfiderable army of our foes is led by *Bheem.* Let all the generals, according to their refpective divifions, ftand in their pofts, and one and all refolve *Bheefhma* to fupport."

The ancient chief[1], and brother of the grandfire of the *Kooroos,* then, fhouting with a voice like a roaring lion, blew his fhell[2] to raife the fpirits of the *Kooroo* chief; and inftantly innumerable fhells, and other warlike inftruments, were ftruck up on all fides, fo that the clangour was exceffive. At this time *Kreefhna*[3] and *Arjoon*[4] were ftanding in a fplendid chariot drawn by white horfes. They alfo founded their fhells, which were of celeftial form: the name of the one which was blown by *Kreefhna,* was *Panchajanya,* and that of *Arjoon* was called *Deva-datta. Bheem,* of dreadful deeds, blew his capacious fhell *Powndra,* and *Yoodheefhteer,* the royal fon of *Koontee,* founded *Ananta-Veejay. Nakool* and *Sahadeva* blew their fhells alfo; the one called *Soogofha,* the other

other *Maneepooſhpaka.* The prince of *Kaſee* of the mighty bow, *Seekhandee, Dhreeſhtadhoₑmna, Veerata, Satyakee* of invincible arm, *Droopad* and the ſons of his royal daughter *Kreeſhna,* with the ſon of *Soobhadra,* and all the other chiefs and nobles, blew alſo their reſpective ſhells; ſo that their ſhrill ſounding voices pierced the hearts of the *Kooroos,* and re-echoed with a dreadful noiſe from heaven to earth.

In the mean time *Arjoon,* perceiving that the ſons of *Dhreetaraſhtra* ſtood ready to begin the fight, and that the weapons began to fly abroad, having taken up his bow, addreſſed *Kreeſhna* in the following words:

ARJOON.

" I pray thee, *Kreeſhna,* cauſe my chariot to be driven and placed between the two armies, that I may behold who are the men that ſtand ready, anxious to commence the bloody fight; and with whom it is that I am to fight in this ready field; and who they are that are here aſſembled to ſupport the vindictive ſon of *Dhreetaraſhtra* in the battle."

Kreeſhna being thus addreſſed by *Arjoon,* drove the chariot; and, having cauſed it to halt in the midſt of the ſpace in front of the two armies, bad *Arjoon* caſt his eyes towards the ranks of the *Kooroos,* and behold where ſtood the aged *Bheeſhma,* and *Dron,* with all the chief nobles of their party. He looked at both the armies, and beheld, on either ſide, none but grandſires, uncles, couſins, tutors, ſons, and brothers, near relations, or boſom friends; and when he had gazed for a while, and beheld ſuch friends as theſe prepared for the fight, he was ſeized with extreme pity and compunction, and uttered his ſorrow in the following words:

ARJOON.

" Having beheld, O *Kreeſhna!* my kindred thus ſtanding anxious for the fight, my members fail me, my coun-

4   tenance

tenance withereth, the hair ftandeth an end upon my
body, and all my frame trembleth with horror! Even
Gandeev my bow efcapeth from my hand, and my fkin is
parched and dried up. I am not able to ftand; for my
underftanding, as it were, turneth round, and I behold
inaufpicious omens on all fides. When I fhall have deftroyed my kindred, fhall I longer look for happinefs? I
wifh not for victory, *Kreefhna*; I want not dominion; I
want not pleafure; for what is dominion, and the enjoyments of life, or even life itfelf, when thofe, for whom
dominion, pleafure, and enjoyment were to be coveted,
have abandoned life and fortune, and ftand here in the
field ready for the battle? Tutors, fons and fathers,
grandfires and grandfons, uncles and nephews, coufins,
kindred, and friends! Although they would kill me, I
wifh not to fight them; no not even for the dominion of
the three regions of the univerfe, much lefs for this little
earth! Having killed the fons of *Dhreetarafhtra*, what
pleafure, O *Kreefhna*, can we enjoy? Should we deftroy
them, tyrants as they are, fin would take refuge with us.
It therefore behoveth us not to kill fuch near relations as
thefe. How, O *Kreefhna*, can we be happy hereafter,
when we have been the murderers of our race? What if
they, whofe minds are depraved by the luft of power, fee
no fin in the extirpation of their race, no crime in the
murder of their friends, is that a reafon why we fhould
not refolve to turn away from fuch a crime, we who ab-
hor the fin of extirpating the kindred of our blood! In
the deftruction of a family, the ancient virtue of the family is loft. Upon the lofs of virtue, vice and impiety
overwhelm the whole of a race. From the influence
of impiety the females of a family grow vicious; and
from women that are become vicious are born the fpurious brood called *Varna-fankar*. The *Sankar* provideth
Hell[s] both for thofe which are flain and thofe which
                                                    furvive;

furvive; and their forefathers[6], being deprived of the ceremonies of cakes and water offered to their manes, fink
into the infernal regions.   By the crimes of thofe who
murder their own relations, fore caufe of contamination
and birth of *Varna-fankars*, the family virtue, and the
virtue of a whole tribe is for ever done away; and we
have been told, O *Kreefhna*, that the habitation of thofe
mortals whofe generation hath loft its virtue, fhall be in
Hell.   Woe is me! what a great crime are we prepared
to commit! Alas! that for the luft of the enjoyments of
dominion we ftand here ready to murder the kindred of
our own blood! I would rather patiently fuffer that the
fons of *Dhreetarafhtra*, with their weapons in their
hands, fhould come upon me, and, unoppofed, kill me
unguarded in the field."

When *Arjoon* had ceafed to fpeak, he fat down in the
chariot between the two armies; and having put away
his bow and arrows, his heart was overwhelmed with af-
flidion.

LECTURE

LECTURE II.

OF THE NATURE OF THE SOUL, AND SPECULATIVE DOCTRINES.

KREESHNA beholding him thus influenced by compunction, his eyes overflowing with a flood of tears, and his heart oppreſſed with deep affliction, addreſſed him in the following words:

KREESHNA.

"Whence, O *Arjoon*, cometh unto thee, thus ſtanding in the field of battle, this folly and unmanly weakneſs? It is diſgraceful, contrary to duty[7], and the foundation of diſhonour. Yield not thus to unmanlineſs, for it ill becometh one like thee. Abandon this deſpicable weakneſs of thy heart, and ſtand up."

ARJOON.

"How, O *Kreeſhna*, ſhall I reſolve to fight with my arrows in the field againſt ſuch as *Bheeſhma* and *Dron*, who, of all men, are moſt worthy of my reſpect? I would rather beg my bread about the world, than be the murderer of my preceptors, to whom ſuch awful reverence is due. Should I deſtroy ſuch friends as theſe, I ſhould partake of poſſeſſions, wealth, and pleaſures, polluted with their blood. We know not whether it would be better that we ſhould defeat them, or they us; for thoſe, whom having killed, I ſhould not wiſh to live, are even the ſons and people of *Dhreetaraſhtra* who are here drawn up before us. My compaſſionate nature is overcome by the dread of ſin.

Tell me truly what may be beſt for me to do. I am thy diſciple, wherefore inſtruct me in my duty, who am under thy tuition; for my underſtanding is confounded

by

by the dictates of my duty[1], and I see nothing that may assuage the grief which drieth up my faculties, although I were to obtain a kingdom without a rival upon earth, or dominion over the hosts of heaven."

Arjoon having thus spoken to *Kreeshna*, and declared that he would not fight, was silent. *Kreeshna* smiling, addressed the afflicted prince, standing in the midst of the two armies, in the following words:

KREESHNA.

"Thou grievest for those who are unworthy to be lamented, whilst thy sentiments are those of the wise men[9]. The wise neither grieve for the dead nor for the living. I myself never *was not*, nor thou, nor all the princes of the earth; nor shall we ever hereafter cease *to be*. As the soul in this mortal frame findeth infancy, youth, and old age; so, in some future frame, will it find the like. One who is confirmed in this belief, is not disturbed by any thing that may come to pass. The sensibility of the faculties giveth heat and cold, pleasure and pain; which come and go, and are transient and inconstant. Bear them with patience, O son of *Bharat*; for the wise man, whom these disturb not, and to whom pain and pleasure are the same, is formed for immortality. A thing imaginary hath no existence, whilst that which is true is a stranger to non-entity. By those who look into the principles of things, the design of each is seen. Learn that he by whom all things were formed is incorruptible, and that no one is able to effect the destruction of this thing which is inexhaustible. These bodies, which envelope the souls which inhabit them, which are eternal, incorruptible, and surpassing all conception, are declared to be finite beings; wherefore, O *Arjoon*, resolve to fight. The man who believeth that it is the soul which killeth, and he who thinketh that the soul may be destroyed, are both alike deceived; for it neither killeth, nor is it killed. It

is

is not a thing of which a man may fay, it hath been, it
is about to be, or is to be hereafter; for it is a thing
without birth; it is ancient, conftant, and eternal,
and is not to be deftroyed in this its mortal frame.
How can the man, who believeth that this thing is incorruptible, eternal, inexhauftible, and without birth, think
that he can either kill or caufe it to be killed?. As a man
throweth away old garments, and putteth on new, even
fo the foul, having quitted its old mortal frames, entereth
into others which are new. The weapon divideth it not,
the fire burneth it not, the water corrupteth it not, the
wind drieth it not away; for it is indivifible, inconfu-
mable, incorruptible, and is not to be dried away: it is
eternal, univerfal, permanent, immoveable; it is invifible,
inconceivable, and unalterable; therefore, believing it
to be thus, thou fhouldft not grieve. But whether thou
believeft it of eternal birth and duration, or that it dieth
with the body, ftill thou haft no caufe to lament it.
Death is certain to all things which are fubject to birth,
and regeneration to all things which are mortal; wherefore it doth not behove thee to grieve about that which
is inevitable. The former ftate of beings is unknown;
the middle ftate is evident, and their future ftate is not
to be difcovered. Why then fhouldft thou trouble thyfelf about fuch things as thefe? Some regard the foul as
a wonder, whilft fome fpeak, and others hear of it with
aftonifhment; but no one knoweth it, although he may
have heard it defcribed. This fpirit being never to be
deftroyed in the mortal frame which it inhabiteth, it is
unworthy for thee to be troubled for all thefe mortals.
Caft but thy eyes towards the duties of thy particular
tribe, and it will ill become thee to tremble. A foldier
of the *Kfhatree* tribe hath no duty fuperior to fighting.
Juft to thy wifh the door of heaven is found open before
thee. Such foldiers only as are the favorites of Heaven

obtain

obtain fuch a glorious fight as this. But, if thou wilt
not perform the duty of thy calling, and fight out the
field, thou wilt abandon thy duty and thy honor, and be
guilty of a crime. Mankind fpeak of thy renown as infinite and inexhauftible. The fame of one who hath
been refpected in the world is extended even beyond the
diffolution. of the body. The generals of the armies will
think that thy retirement from the field arofe from fear,
and thou wilt become defpicable, even amongft thofe by
whom thou wert wont to be refpected. Thy enemies will
fpeak of thee in words which are unworthy to be fpoken,
and depreciate thy courage and abilities: what can be
more dreadful than this! If thou art flain thou wilt
obtain heaven; if thou art victorious thou wilt enjoy a
world for thy reward; wherefore, fon of *Koontee*, arife
and be determined for the battle. Make pleafure and
pain, gain and lofs, victory and defeat, the fame, and then
prepare for battle; or if thou doft not, thou wilt be cri-
minal in a high degree. Let thy reafon be thus applied
in the field of battle.

This thy judgment is formed upon the fpeculative doctrines of the *Sankhya faftra*; hear what it is in the practical, with which being endued thou fhalt forfake the
bonds of action[10]. A very fmall portion of this duty de-
livereth a man from great fear. In this there is but one
judgment; but that is of a definite nature, whilft the
judgments of thofe of indefinite principles are infinite
and of many branches.

Men of confined notions, delighting in the controver-
fies of the *Veds*, tainted with worldly lufts, and preferring
a tranfient enjoyment of heaven to eternal abforption,
whilft they declare there is no other reward, pronounce,
for the attainment of worldly riches and enjoyments,
flowery fentences, ordaining innumerable and manifold
ceremonies, and promifing rewards for the actions of this
life.

life. The determined judgment of such as are attached
to riches and enjoyment, and whose reason is led astray
by this doctrine, is not formed upon mature consideration
and meditation. The objects of the *Veds* are of a threefold nature[11]. Be thou free from a threefold nature; be
free from duplicity, and stand firm in the path of truth;
be free from care and trouble, and turn thy mind to
things which are spiritual. The knowing divine findeth
as many uses in the whole *Veds* collectively, as in a re-
servoir full flowing with water.

Let the motive be in the deed, and not in the event.
Be not one whose motive for action is the hope of reward. Let not thy life be spent in inaction. Depend
upon application, perform thy duty, abandon all thought
of the consequence, and make the event equal, whether
it terminate in good or evil; for such an equality is called
Yog[12]. The action stands at a distance inferior to the application of wisdom. Seek an asylum then in wisdom[13]
alone; for the miserable and unhappy are so on account
of the event of things. Men who are endued with true
wisdom are unmindful of good or evil in this world.
Study then to obtain this application of thy understanding, for such application in business is a precious art.

Wise men, who have abandoned all thought of the
fruit which is produced from their actions, are freed from
the chains of birth, and go to the regions of eternal hap-
piness.

When thy reason shall get the better of the gloomy
weakness of thy heart, then shalt thou have attained all
knowledge which hath been or is worthy to be taught.
When thy understanding, by study brought to maturity,
shall be fixed immoveably in contemplation, then shall it
obtain true wisdom."

ARJOON.

What, O *Kreeshna*, is the distinction of that wise and
steady

fteady man who is fixed in contemplation? What may
fuch a fage declare? Where may he dwell? How may
he act?

KREESHNA.

A man is faid to be confirmed in wifdom, when he
forfaketh every defire which entereth into his heart, and
of himfelf is happy, and contented in himfelf. His mind
is undifturbed in adverfity, he is happy and contented
in profperity, and he is a ftranger to anxiety, fear, and
anger. Such a wife man is called a *Moonee*. The wifdom of that man is eftablifhed, who in all things is
without affection; and, having received good or evil,
neither rejoiceth at the one, nor is caft down by the
other. His wifdom is confirmed, when, like the tortoife, he can draw in all his members, and reftrain them
from their wonted purpofes. The hungry man lofeth
every other object but the gratification of his appetite,
and when he is become acquainted with the Supreme, he
lofeth even that. The tumultuous fenfes hurry away,
by force, the heart even of the wife man who ftriveth
to reftrain them. The infpired man, trufting in me,
may quell them and be happy. The man who hath his
paffions in fubjection, is poffeffed of true wifdom.

The man who attendeth to the inclinations of the
fenfes, in them hath a concern; from this concern is
created paffion, from paffion anger, from anger is produced folly[14], from folly a depravation of the memory,
from the lofs of memory the lofs of reafon, and from
the lofs of reafon the lofs of all! A man of a govern-
able mind, enjoying the objects of his fenfes, with all
his faculties rendered obedient to his will, and freed
from pride and malice, obtaineth happinefs fupreme. In
this happinefs is born to him an exemption from all his
troubles; and his mind being thus at eafe, wifdom
prefently floweth to him from all fides. The man who

5   attendeth

attendeth not to this, is without wifdom or the power of contemplation. The man who is incapable of thinking, hath no reft. What happinefs can he enjoy who hath no reft? The heart, which followeth the dictates of the moving paffions, carrieth away his reafon, as the ftorm the bark in the raging ocean. The man, therefore, who can reftrain all his paffions from their inordinate defires, is endued with true wifdom. Such a one walketh but in that night when all things go to reft, the night of *time*. The contemplative *Moonee* fleepeth but in the day of *time*, when all things wake.

The man whofe paffions enter his heart as waters run into the unfwelling paffive ocean, obtaineth happinefs; not he who lufteth in his lufts. The man who, having abandoned all lufts of the flefh, walketh without inordinate defires, unaffuming, and free from pride, obtaineth happinefs. This is divine dependence. A man being poffeffed of this confidence in the Supreme, goeth not aftray: even at the hour of death, fhould he attain it, he fhall mix with the incorporeal nature of *Brahm*.

LECTURE

LECTURE III.

OF WORKS.

ARJOON.

IF, according to thy opinion, the ufe of the underftanding be fuperior to the practice of deeds", why
then doft thou urge me to engage in an undertaking fo
dreadful as this? Thou, as it were, confoundeft my
reafon with a mixture of fentiments; wherefore choofe
one amongft them, by which I may obtain happinefs,
and explain it unto me.

KREESHNA.

It hath before been obferved by me, that in this world
there are two inftitutes: That of thofe who follow the
Sankhya, or fpeculative fcience, which is the exercife of
reafon in contemplation; and the practical, or exercife
of the moral and religious duties.

The man enjoyeth not freedom from action, from the
non-commencement of that which he hath to do; nor
doth he obtain happinefs from a total inactivity. No
one ever refteth a moment inactive. Every man is
involuntarily urged to act by thofe principles which are
inherent in his nature. The man who reftraineth his
active faculties, and fitteth down with his mind attentive to the objects of his fenfes, is called one of an
aftrayed foul, and the practifer of deceit. So the man
is praifed, who, having fubdued all his paffions, performeth with his active faculties all the functions of life,
unconcerned about the event. Perform the fettled
functions: action is preferable to inaction. The journey of thy mortal frame may not fucceed from inaction.
This bufy world is engaged from other motives than the
worfhip

worſhip of the Deity. Abandon then, O ſon of *Koontee*,
all ſelfiſh motives, and perform thy duty for him alone.

When in ancient days *Brabma*[16], the lord of the creation, had formed mankind, and, at the ſame time, appointed his worſhip, he ſpoke and ſaid : " With this
" worſhip pray for increaſe, and let it be that on which
" ye ſhall depend for the accompliſhment of all your
" wiſhes. With this remember the Gods, that the
" Gods may remember you. Remember one another,
" and ye ſhall obtain ſupreme happineſs. The Gods
" being remembered in worſhip, will grant you the
" enjoyment of your wiſhes. He who enjoyeth what
" hath been given unto him by them, and offereth not
" a portion unto them, is even as a thief. Thoſe who
" eat not but what is left of the offerings, shall be
" purified of all their tranſgreſſions. Thoſe who dreſs
" their meat but for themſelves, eat the bread of ſin.
" All things which have life are generated from the
" bread which they eat. Bread is generated from rain ;
" rain from divine worſhip, and divine worſhip from
" good works. Know that good works come from
" *Brabm,* whoſe nature is incorruptible ; wherefore the
" omnipreſent *Brabm* is preſent in the worſhip."

The ſinful mortal, who delighteth in the gratification
of his paſſions, and followeth not the wheel, thus revolving in the world, liveth but in vain.

But the man who may be ſelf-delighted and ſelf-
ſatisfied, and who may be happy in his own ſoul,
hath no occaſion[17]. He hath no intereſt either in that
which is done, or that which is not done; and there
is not, in all things which have been created, any object on which he may place dependence. Wherefore,
perform thou that which thou haſt to do, at all times, unmindful of the event; for the man that doeth that which
he hath to do, without affection, obtaineth the Supreme.

Janaka

Janaka and others have attained perfection[18] even by works. Thou fhouldft alfo obferve what is the practice of mankind, and act accordingly. The man of low degree followeth the example of him who is above him, and doeth that which he doeth. I myfelf, *Arjoon*, have not, in the three regions of the univerfe, any thing which is neceffary for me to perform, nor any thing to obtain which is not obtained; and yet I live in the exercife of the moral duties. If I were not vigilantly to attend to thefe duties, all men would prefently follow my example. If I were not to perform the moral actions, this world would fail in their duty; I fhould be the caufe of fpurious births, and fhould drive the people from the right way. As the ignorant perform the duties of life from the hope of reward, fo the wife man, out of refpect to the opinions and prejudices of mankind, fhould perform the fame without motives of intereft. He fhould not create a divifion in the underftandings of the ignorant, who are inclined to outward works. The learned man, by induftrioufly performing all the duties of life, fhould induce the vulgar to attend to them.

The man whofe mind is led aftray by the pride of felf-fufficiency, thinketh that he himfelf is the executor of all thofe actions which are performed by the principles of his conftitution. But the man who is acquainted with the nature of the two diftinctions of caufe and effect, having confidered that principles will act according to their natures, giveth himfelf no trouble. Men who are led aftray by the principles of their natures, are interefted in the works of the faculties. The man who is acquainted with the whole, fhould not drive thofe from their works who are flow of comprehenfion, and lefs experienced than himfelf.

Throw every deed on me, and with a heart, over
which

which the foul prefideth, be free from hope, be unpre-
fuming, be free from trouble, and refolve to fight.

Thofe who with a firm belief, and without reproach,
fhall conftantly follow this my doctrine, fhall be faved
even by works; and know that thofe who, holding it in
contempt, follow not this my counfel, are aftrayed from
all wifdom, deprived of reafon, and are loft.

But the wife man alfo feeketh for that which is homo-
geneous to his own nature. All things act according to
their natures, what then will reftraint effect? In every
purpofe of the fenfes are fixed affection and diflike. A
wife man fhould not put himfelf in their power, for
both of them are his opponents. A man's own religion,
though contrary to, is better than the faith of another,
let it be ever fo well followed. It is good to die in one's
own faith, for another's faith beareth fear.

A R J O O N.

By what, O *Kreefhna*, is man compelled to commit
offences? He feems as if, contrary to his wifhes, he
was impelled by fome fecret force.

K R E E S H N A.

Know that it is the enemy luft, or paffion, offspring
of the carnal principle, infatiable and full of fin, by
which this world is covered as the flame by the fmoke,
as the mirror by ruft, or as the fœtus by its membrane.
The underftanding of the wife man is obfcured by this
inveterate foe, in the fhape of defire[19], who rageth like
fire, and is hard to be appeafed. It is faid that the
fenfes, the heart, and the underftanding are the places
where he delighteth moft to rule. By the affiftance of
thefe he overwhelmeth reafon, and ftupefieth the foul.
Thou fhouldft, therefore, firft fubdue thy paffions, and
get the better of this finful deftroyer of wifdom and
knowledge.

The organs are efteemed great, but the mind is greater
than

han they. The refolution[20] is greater than the mind, and who is fuperior to the refolution is *he*[21]. When thou haft refolved what is fuperior to the refolution, and fixed thyfelf by thyfelf, determine to abandon the enemy in the fhape of defire, whose objects are hard to be accomplifhed.

LECTURE

LECTURE IV.

OF THE FORSAKING OF WORKS.

KREESHNA.

THIS never-failing difcipline I formerly taught unto *Veevafwat*, and *Veevafwat* communicated it to *Manoo*, and *Manoo* made it known unto *Eekſhwakoo*; and being delivered down from one unto another, it was ftudied by the *Rajarſhees*; until at length, in the courfe of time, the mighty art was loft. It is even the fame difcipline which I have this day communicated unto thee, becaufe thou art my fervant and my friend. It is an ancient and a fupreme myftery.

ARJOON.

Seeing thy birth is pofterior to the life of *Eekſhwakoo*, how am I to underftand that thou hadft been formerly the teacher of this doctrine?

KREESHNA.

Both I and thou have paffed many births. Mine are known unto me; but thou knoweft not of thine.

Although I am not in my nature fubject to birth or decay, and am the lord of all created beings; yet, having command over my own nature, I am made evident by my own power; and as often as there is a decline of virtue, and an infurrection of vice and injuftice, in the world, I make myfelf evident; and thus I appear, from age to age, for the prefervation of the juft, the deftruction of the wicked, and the eftablifhment of virtue.

He, O *Arjoon*, who, from conviction, acknowledgeth my divine birth and actions to be even fo, doth not, upon his quitting his mortal frame, enter into another, for he entereth into me. Many who were free from affection,

affection, fear, and anger, and, filled with my fpirit, depended upon me, having been purified by the power of wifdom, have entered into me. I affift thofe men who in all things walk in my path, even as they ferve me.

Thofe who wifh for fuccefs to their works in this life, worfhip the *Devatas*[11]. That which is achieved in this life, from works, fpeedily cometh to pafs.

Mankind was created by me of four kinds, diftinct in their principles, and in their duties. Know me then to be the creator of mankind, uncreated, and without decay.

Works affect not me, nor have I any expectations from the fruits of works. He who believeth me to be even fo, is not bound by works. The ancients, who longed for eternal falvation, having difcovered this, ftill performed works. Wherefore perform thou works, even as they were performed by the ancients in former times. The learned even are puzzled to determine what is work, and what is not. I will tell thee what that work is, by knowing which thou wilt be delivered from misfortune. It may be defined—action, improper action, and inaction. The path of action is full of darknefs.

He who may behold, as it were, *inaction* in action, and *action* in inaction, is wife amongft mankind. He is a perfect performer of all duty.

Wife men call him a *Pandeet*, whofe every undertaking is free from the idea of defire, and whofe actions are confumed by the fire of wifdom. He abandoneth the defire of a reward of his actions; he is always contented and independent; and although he may be engaged in a work, he, as it were, doeth nothing. He is unfolicitous, of a fubdued mind and fpirit, and exempt from every perception; and, as he doeth only the

6   offices

offices of the body, he committeth no offence. He is
pleafed with whatever he may by chance obtain; he
hath gotten the better of duplicity, and he is free from
envy. He is the fame in profperity and adverfity; and
although he acteth, he is not confined in the action. The
work of him, who hath loft all anxiety for the event,
who is freed from the bonds of action, and ftandeth
with his mind fubdued by fpiritual wifdom, and who
performeth it for the fake of worfhip, cometh altogether
unto nothing. God is the gift of charity; God is the
offering; God is in the fire of the altar; by God is the
facrifice performed; and God is to be obtained by him
who maketh God alone the object of his works.

Some of the devout attend to the worfhip of the
Devatas, or angels; others, with offerings, direct their
worfhip unto God in the fire; others facrifice their ears,
and other organs, in the fire of conftraint; whilft fome
facrifice found, and the like, in the fire of their organs.
Some again facrifice the actions of all their organs and
faculties in the fire of felf-conftraint, lighted up by the
fpark of infpired wifdom. There are alfo the worfhippers with offerings, and the worfhippers with mortifications; and again the worfhippers with enthufiastic
devotion; fo there are thofe, the wifdom of whofe reading is their worfhip, men of fubdued paffions and fevere
manners. Some there are who facrifice their breathing
fpirit, and force it downwards from its natural course;
whilft others force the fpirit which is below back with
the breath; and a few, with whom thefe two faculties
are held in great efteem, clofe up the door of each; and
there are fome, who eat but by rule, who facrifice their
lives in their lives. All thefe different kinds of worfhippers are, by their particular modes of worfhip, purified
from their offences. He who enjoyeth but the *Amreeta*
which is left of his offerings, obtaineth the eternal fpirit
of

of *Brahm*, the fupreme. This world is not for him who doeth not worſhip; and where, O *Arjoon*, is there another[21]?

A great variety of modes of worſhip like theſe are diſplayed in the mouth of God. Learn that they are all the offsprings of action. Being convinced of this, thou ſhalt obtain an eternal releaſe; for know that the worſhip of ſpiritual wiſdom is far better than the worſhip with offerings of things. In wiſdom is to be found every work without exception. Seek then this wiſdom with proſtrations, with queſtions, and with attention, that thoſe learned men who ſee its principles may inſtruct thee in its rules; which having learnt, thou ſhalt not again, O ſon of *Pandoo*, fall into folly; by which thou ſhalt behold all nature in the ſpirit; that is, in me[24]. Although thou wert the greateſt of all offenders, thou ſhalt be able to croſs the gulf of ſin with the bark of wiſdom. As the natural fire, O *Arjoon*, reduceth the wood to aſhes, ſo may the fire of wiſdom reduce all moral actions to aſhes. There is not any thing in this world to be compared with wiſdom for purity. He who is perfected by practice, in due time findeth it in his own ſoul. He who hath faith findeth wiſdom; and, above all, he who hath gotten the better of his paſſions; and having obtained this ſpiritual wiſdom, he ſhortly enjoyeth ſuperior happineſs; whilſt the ignorant, and the man without faith, whoſe ſpirit is full of doubt, is loſt. Neither this world, nor that which is above, nor happineſs, can be enjoyed by the man of a doubting mind. The human actions have no power to confine[25] the ſpiritual mind, which, by ſtudy, hath forſaken works, and which, by wiſdom, hath cut aſunder the bonds of doubt. Wherefore, O ſon of *Bharat*, reſolve to cut aſunder this doubt, offſpring of ignorance, which hath taken poſſeſſion of thy mind, with the edge of the wiſdom of thy own ſoul, and ariſe and attach thyſelf to the diſcipline.

LECTURE

LECTURE V.

OF FORSAKING THE FRUITS OF WORKS.

ARJOON.

THOU now fpeakeft, O *Kreefhna*, of the forfaking of works, and now again of performing them. Tell me pofitively which of the two is beft.

KREESHNA.

Both the defertion and the practice of works are equally the means of extreme happinefs; but of the two the practice of works is to be diftinguifhed above the defertion. The perpetual reclufe, who neither longeth nor complaineth, is worthy to be known. Such a one is free from duplicity, and is happily freed from the bond of action. Children only, and not the learned, fpeak of the fpeculative and the practical doctrines as two. They are but one, for both obtain the felf-fame end, and the place which is gained by the followers of the one, is gained by the followers of the other. That man feeth, who feeth that the fpeculative doctrines and the practical are but one. To be a *Sannyafee*, or reclufe, without application, is to obtain pain and trouble; whilft the *Moonee*, who is employed in the practice of his duty, prefently obtaineth *Brahm*, the Almighty. The man who, employed in the practice of works, is of a purified foul, a fubdued fpirit, and reftrained paffions, and whofe foul is the univerfal foul, is not affected by fo being. The attentive man, who is acquainted with the principles of things, in feeing, hearing, touching, fmelling, eating, moving, fleeping, breathing, talking, quitting, taking, opening and clofing his eyes, thinketh that he doeth nothing; but that the faculties are only employed

ployed in their feveral objects. The man who, performing the duties of life, and quitting all intereft in them,
placeth them upon *Brahm*, the Supreme, is not tainted
by fin; but remaineth like the leaf of the lotus unaffected by the waters. Practical men, who perform the
offices of life but with their bodies, their minds, their
underftandings, and their fenfes, and forfake the confequence for the purification of their fouls; and, although
employed, forfake the fruit of action, obtain infinite
happinefs; whilft the man who is unemployed, being
attached to the fruit by the agent defire, is in the bonds
of confinement. The man who hath his paffions in fubjection, and with his mind forfaketh all works, his foul
fitteth at reft in the nine-gate city of its abode[26], neither
acting nor caufing to act.

The Almighty createth neither the powers nor the
deeds of mankind[27], nor the application of the fruits of
action: nature prevaileth. The Almighty receiveth
neither the vices nor the virtues of any one. Mankind
are led aftray by their reafons being obfcured by ignorance; but when that ignorance of their fouls is deftroyed
by the force of reafon, their wifdom fhineth forth again
with the glory of the fun, and caufeth the Deity to
appear. Thofe whofe underftandings are in him, whofe
fouls are in him, whofe confidence is in him, and whofe
afylum is in him, are by wifdom purified from all their
offences, and go from whence they fhall never return.

The learned behold him alike in the reverend *Brahman* perfected in knowledge, in the ox, and in the elephant; in the dog, and in him who eateth of the flefh
of dogs. Thofe whofe minds are fixed on this equality,
gain eternity even in this world. They put their truft
in *Brahm*, the Eternal, becaufe he is every where alike,
free from fault.

The man who knoweth *Brahm*, and confideth in

Brahm,

Brahm, and whofe mind is fteady and free from folly,
fhould neither rejoice in profperity, nor complain in adverfity. He whofe foul is unaffected by the impreffions
made upon the outward feelings, obtaineth what is pleafure in his own mind. Such an one, whofe foul is thus
fixed upon the ftudy of *Brahm*, enjoyeth pleafure without
decline. The enjoyments which proceed from the feelings are as the wombs of future pain. The wife man,
who is acquainted with the beginning and the end of
things, delighteth not in thefe. He who can bear up
againft the violence which is produced from luft and
anger in this mortal life, is properly employed and a
happy man. The man who is happy in his heart, at
reft in his mind, and enlightened within, is a *Yogee*, or
one devoted to God, and of a godly fpirit ; and obtaineth the immaterial nature of *Brahm*, the Supreme.
Such *Reeſhees* as are purified from their offences, freed
from doubt, of fubdued minds, and interefted in the
good of all mankind, obtain the incorporeal *Brahm*.
The incorporeal *Brahm* is prepared, from the beginning,
for fuch as are free from luft and anger, of humble
minds and fubdued fpirits, and who are acquainted with
their own fouls.

The man who keepeth the outward accidents from
entering his mind, and his eyes fixed in contemplation
between his brows ; who maketh the breath to pafs
through both his noftrils alike in expiration and infpiration ; who is of fubdued faculties, mind, and underftanding, and hath fet his heart upon falvation ; and
who is free from luft, fear, and anger, is for ever bleffed
in this life ; and, being convinced that I am the cherifher
of religious zeal, the lord of all worlds, and the friend
of all nature, he fhall obtain me and be bleffed.

LECTURE

LECTURE VI.

OF THE EXERCISE OF SOUL.

KREESHNA.

HE is both a *Yogee* and a *Sannyasee* who performeth that which he hath to do independent of the fruit thereof; not he who liveth without the facrificial fire and without action. Learn, O fon of *Pandoo*, that what they call *Sannyas*, or a forfaking of the world, is the fame with *Yog* or the practice of devotion. He cannot be a *Yogee*, who, in his actions, hath not abandoned all intentions. Works are faid to be the means by which a man who wifheth, may attain devotion; fo reft is called the means for him who hath attained devotion. When the all-contemplative *Sannyasee* is not engaged in the objects of the fenfes, nor in works, then he is called one who hath attained devotion. He fhould raife himfelf by himfelf: he fhould not fuffer his foul to be depreffed. Self is the friend of felf; and, in like manner, felf is its own enemy. Self is the friend of him by whom the fpirit is fubdued with the fpirit; fo felf, like a foe, delighteth in the enmity of him who hath no foul. The foul of the placid conquered fpirit is the fame collected in heat and cold, in pain and pleafure, in honor and difgrace. The man whofe mind is replete with divine wifdom and learning, who ftandeth upon the pinnacle, and hath fubdued his paffions, is faid to be devout. To the *Yogee*, gold, iron, and ftones, are the fame. The man is diftinguifhed whofe refolutions, whether amongft his companions and friends; in the midft of enemies, or thofe who ftand aloof or go between; with thofe who love and thofe who hate; in the company of faints or finners, is the fame.

The

The *Yogee* conftantly exercifeth the fpirit in private.
He is reclufe, of a fubdued mind and fpirit; free from
hope, and free from perception. He planteth his own
feat firmly on a fpot that is undefiled, neither too high
nor too low, and fitteth upon the facred grafs which is
called *Koos,* covered with a fkin and a cloth. There he,
whofe bufinefs is the reftraining of his paffions, fhould
fit, with his mind fixed on one object alone, in the exercife of his devotion for the purification of his foul,
keeping his head, his neck, and body, fteady without
motion, his eyes fixed on the point of his nofe, looking
at no other place around. The peaceful foul, releafed
from fear, who would keep in the path of one who followeth God, fhould reftrain the mind, and, fixing it on
me, depend on me alone. The *Yogee* of an humbled
mind, who thus conftantly exercifeth his foul, obtaineth
happinefs incorporeal and fupreme in me.

This divine difcipline, *Arjoon,* is not to be attained
by him who eateth more than enough, or lefs than
enough; neither by him who hath a habit of fleeping
much, nor by him who fleepeth not at all. The difcipline which deftroyeth pain belongeth to him who is
moderate in eating and in recreation, whofe inclinations
are moderate in action, and who is moderate in fleep.
A man is called devout when his mind remaineth thus
regulated within himfelf, and he is exempt from every
luft and inordinate defire. The *Yogee* of a fubdued
mind, thus employed in the exercife of his devotion, is
compared to a lamp, ftanding in a place without wind,
which waveth not. He delighteth in his own foul,
where the mind, regulated by the fervice of devotion, is
pleafed to dwell, and where, by the affiftance of the fpirit,
he beholdeth the foul. He becometh acquainted with
that boundlefs pleafure which is far more worthy of the
underftanding than that which arifeth from the fenses;
depending

depending upon which, the mind moveth not from its principles; which having obtained, he refpecteth no other acquifition fo great as it; in which depending, he is not moved by the fevereft pain. This difunion from the conjunction of pain may be diftinguifhed by the appellation *Yog*, fpiritual union or devotion. It is to be attained by refolution, by the man who knoweth his own mind. When he hath abandoned every defire that arifeth from the imagination, and fubdued with his mind every inclination of the fenfes, he may, by degrees, find reft; and having, by a fteady refolution, fixed his mind within himfelf, he fhould think of nothing elfe. Wherefoever the unfteady mind roameth, he fhould fubdue it, bring it back, and place it in his own breaft. Supreme happinefs attendeth the man whofe mind is thus at peace; whofe carnal affections and paffions are thus fubdued; who is thus in God, and free from fin. The man who is thus conftantly in the exercife of the foul, and free from fin, enjoyeth eternal happinefs, united with *Brahm* the Supreme. The man whofe mind is endued with this devotion, and looketh on all things alike, beholdeth the fupreme foul in all things, and all things in the fupreme foul. He who beholdeth me in all things, and beholdeth all things in me, I forfake not him, and he forfaketh not me. The *Yogee* who believeth in unity, and worfhippeth me prefent in all things, dwelleth in me in all refpects, even whilft he liveth. The man, O *Arjoon*, who, from what paffeth in his own breaft, whether it be pain or pleafure, beholdeth the fame in others, is efteemed a fupreme *Yogee*.

ARJOON.

From the reftleffnefs of our natures, I conceive not the permanent duration of this doctrine of equality which thou haft told me. The mind, O *Kreefhna*, is

7   naturally

naturally unfteady, turbulent, ftrong, and ftubborn. I efteem it as difficult to reftrain as the wind.

KREESHNA.

The mind, O valiant youth, is undoubtedly unfteady, and difficult to be confined; yet, I think it may be reftrained by practice and temperance. In my opinion, this divine difcipline which is called *Yog* is hard to be attained by him who hath not his foul in fubjection; but it may be acquired by him who taketh pains, and hath his foul in his own power.

ARJOON.

Whither, O *Kreefhna*, doth the man go after death, who, although he be endued with faith, hath not obtained perfection in his devotion, becaufe his unfubdued mind wandered from the difcipline? Doth not the fool who is found not ftanding in the path of *Brahm*, and is thus, as it were, fallen between good and evil, like a broken cloud, come to nothing? Thou, *Kreefhna*, canft entirely clear up thefe my doubts; and there is no other perfon to be found able to remove thefe difficulties.

KREESHNA.

His deftruction is found neither here nor in the world above. No man who hath done good goeth unto an evil place. A man whofe devotions have been broken off by death, having enjoyed for an immenfity of years the rewards of his virtues in the regions above, at length is born again in fome holy and refpectable family; or perhaps in the houfe of fome learned *Yogee*. But fuch a regeneration into this life is the moft difficult to attain. Being thus born again, he is endued with the fame degree of application and advancement of his underftanding that he held in his former body; and here he begins again to labour for perfection in devotion. The man[28] who is defirous of learning this devotion, this fpiritual application of the foul, exceedeth even the

word

word of *Brahm*. The *Yogee*, who, labouring with all his might, is purified of his offences, and, after many births, made perfect, at length goeth to the fupreme abode. The *Yogee* is more exalted than *Tapafwees*, thofe zealots who harafs themfelves in performing penances, refpected above the learned in fcience, and fuperior to thofe who are attached to moral works; wherefore, O *Arjoon*, refolve thou to become a *Yogee*. Of all *Yogees*, I refpect him as the moft devout, who hath faith in me, and who ferveth me with a foul poffeffed of my fpirit.

LECTURE

LECTURE VII.

OF THE PRINCIPLES OF NATURE, AND THE VITAL SPIRIT.

KREESHNA.

HEAR, O *Arjoon*, how having thy mind attached to me, being in the exercife of devotion, and making me alone thy afylum, thou wilt, at once, and without doubt, become acquainted with me. I will inftruct thee in this wifdom and learning without referve; which having learnt, there is not in this life any other that is taught worthy to be known.

A few amongft ten thoufand mortals ftrive for perfection; and but a few of thofe who ftrive and become perfect, know me according to my nature. My principle is divided into eight diftinctions: earth, water, fire, air, and æther (*Khang*); together with mind, underftanding, and *Ahang-kar*, (felf-confcioufnefs): but befides this, know that I have another principle diftinct from this, and fuperior, which is of a vital nature[29], and by which this world is fupported. Learn that thefe two are the womb of all nature. I am the creation and the diffolution of the whole univerfe. There is not any thing greater than I; and all things hang on me, even as precious gems upon a ftring. I am moifture in the water, light in the fun and moon, invocation in the *Veds*, found in the firmament, human nature in mankind, fweet-fmelling favor in the earth, glory in the fource of light; in all things I am life, and I am zeal in the zealous; and know, O *Arjoon*, that I am the eternal feed of all nature. I am the underftanding of the wife, the glory of the proud, the ftrength of the ftrong, free from luft

and

and anger; and in animals I am defire regulated by moral fitnefs. But know that I am not in thofe natures which are of the three qualities called *Satwa*, *Raja*, and *Tama*[10], although they proceed from me: yet they are in me. The whole of this world being bewildered by the influence of thefe three-fold qualities, knoweth not that I am diftinct from thefe and without decline. This my divine and fupernatural power, endued with thefe principles and properties, is hard to be overcome. They who come unto me get the better of this fupernatural influence. The wicked, the foolifh, and the low-minded come not unto me, becaufe their underftandings, being bewildered by the fupernatural power, they truft in the principles of evil fpirits.

I am, O *Arjoon*, ferved by four kinds of people who are good: the diftreffed, the inquifitive, the wifhers after wealth[11], and the wife. But of all thefe the wife man, who is conftantly engaged in my fervice, and is a fervant but of one, is the moft diftinguifhed. I am extremely dear to the wife man, and he is dear unto me. All thefe are exalted; but I efteem the wife man even as myfelf, becaufe his devout fpirit dependeth upon me alone as his ultimate refource. The wife man proceedeth not unto me until after many births; for the exalted mind, who believeth that the fon of *Vasoodev* is all, is hard to be found. Thofe whofe underftandings are drawn away by this and that purfuit, go unto other *Devatas*. They depend upon this and that rule of conduct, and are governed by their own principles[12]. Whatever image any fupplicant is defirous of worfhipping in faith, it is I alone who infpire him with that fteady faith; with which being endued, he endeavoureth to render that image propitious, and at length he obtaineth the object of his wifhes as it is appointed by me. But the reward of fuch fhort-fighted men is finite.

Thofe

Thofe who worfhip the *Devatas* go unto them, and thofe who worfhip me alone go unto me. The ignorant, being unacquainted with my fupreme nature, which is fuperior to all things, and exempt from decay, believe me, who am invifible, to exift in the vifible form under which they fee me. I am not vifible to all, becaufe I am concealed by the fupernatural power that is in me. The ignorant world do not difcover this, that I am not fubject to birth or decay. I know, O *Arjoon*, all the beings that have paffed, all that are prefent, and all that fhall hereafter be; but there is not one amongft them who knoweth me. All beings in birth find their reafon fafcinated and perplexed by the wiles of contrary fenfations, arifing from love and hatred. Thofe men of regular lives, whofe fins are done away, being freed from the fafcination arifing from thofe contending paffions, enjoy me. They who put their truft in me, and labour for a deliverance from decay and death, know *Brahm*, the whole *Adhee-atma*, and every *Karma*. The devout fouls who know me to be the *Adhee-bhoot*, the *Adhee-diva*, and the *Adhee-yagna*, know me alfo in the time of their departure.

LECTURE

LECTURE VIII.

OF POOROOSH.

ARJOON.

WHAT is that *Brahm?* What is *Adhee-atma?* What is *Karma*, O firſt of men? What alſo is *Adhee-bhoot* called? What *Adhee-diva?* How is *Adhee-yagna*, and who is here in this body? How art thou to be known in the hour of departure by men of ſubdued minds?

KREESHNA.

Brahm is that which is ſupreme and without corruption; *Adhee-atma* [11] is *Swa-bhab* or particular conſtitution, diſpoſition, quality, or nature; *Karma* is that emanation from which proceedeth the generation of natural beings; *Adhee-bhoot* is the deſtroying nature; *Adhee-diva* is *Pooroofh*; and *Adhee-yagna*, or ſuperintendent of worſhip, is myſelf in this body. At the end of time, he, who having abandoned his mortal frame, departeth thinking only of me, without doubt goeth unto me; or elſe, whatever other nature he ſhall call upon, at the end of life, when he ſhall quit his mortal ſhape, he ſhall ever go unto it. Wherefore at all times think of me alone and fight. Let thy mind and underſtanding be placed in me alone, and thou ſhalt, without doubt, go unto me. The man who longeth after the Divine and Supreme Being, with his mind intent upon the practice of devotion, goeth unto him. The man who ſhall in the laſt hour call upon the ancient Prophet, the prime director, the moſt minute atom, the preſerver of all things, whoſe countenance is like the ſun, and who is diſtinct from darkneſs, with a ſteady mind attached

tached to his fervice, with the force of devotion, and his whole foul fixed between his brows, goeth unto that divine Supreme Being, who is called *Param-Pooroofh*.

I will now fummarily make thee acquainted with that path which the doctors of the *Veds* call never-failing; which the men of fubdued minds and conquered paffions enter; and which, defirous of knowing, they live the lives of *Brahma-charees* or godly pilgrims. He who, having clofed up all the doors of his faculties, locked up his mind in his own breaft, and fixed his fpirit in his head, ftanding firm in the exercife of devotion, re-peating in filence ॐ *Om*[14]*!* the myftic fign of *Brahm*, thence called "*Ekakfhar*," fhall, on his quitting this mortal frame calling upon me, without doubt go the journey of fupreme happinefs. He who thinketh con-ftantly of me, his mind undiverted by another object, I will at all times be eafily found by that conftant ad-herent to devotion; and thofe elevated fouls, who have thus attained fupreme perfection, come unto me, and are no more born in the finite manfion of pain and for-row. Know, O *Arjoon*, that all the regions between this and the abode of *Brahm* afford but a tranfient refi-dence; but he who findeth me, returneth not again to mortal birth.

They who are acquainted with day and night, know that the day of *Brahma* is as a thoufand revolutions of the *Yoogs*[15], and that his night extendeth for a thoufand more. On the coming of that day, all things proceed from invifibility to vifibility; fo, on the approach of night, they are all diffolved away in that which is called *invifible*. The univerfe, even, having exifted, is again diffolved; and now again, on the approach of day, by divine neceffity, it is reproduced. That which, upon the diffolution of all things elfe, is not deftroyed, is fuperior and of another nature from that vifibility: it is

invifible

invisible and eternal. He who is thus called invisible
and incorruptible, is even he who is called the Supreme
Abode; which men having once obtained, they never
more return to earth : that is my mansion. That Supreme Being is to be obtained by him who worshippeth
no other Gods. In him is included all nature ; by him
all things are spread abroad.

I will now speak to thee of that time in which, should
a devout man die, he will never return ; and of that
time, in which dying, he shall return again upon the
earth.

Those holy men who are acquainted with *Brahm*, de-
parting this life in the fiery light of day, in the bright
season of the moon, within the six months of the sun's
northern course, go unto him ; but those who depart in
the gloomy night of the moon's dark season, and whilst
the sun is yet within the southern path of his journey,
ascend for a while into the regions of the moon, and
again return to mortal birth. These two, *light* and
darkness, are esteemed the world's eternal ways : he who
walketh in the former path returneth not; whilst he
who walketh in the latter cometh back again upon the
earth. A *Yogee*, who is acquainted with these two paths
of action, will never be perplexed ; wherefore, O *Arjoon*,
be thou at all times employed in devotion. The fruit
of this surpasseth all the rewards of virtue pointed out
in the *Veds*, in worshippings, in mortifications, and even
in the gifts of charity. The devout *Yogee*, who knoweth
all this, shall obtain a supreme and prior place.

LECTURE

LECTURE IX.

OF THE CHIEF OF SECRETS AND PRINCE OF SCIENCE.

KREESHNA.

I WILL now make known unto thee, who findeſt no fault, a moſt myſterious ſecret, accompanied by profound learning, which having ſtudied thou ſhalt be delivered from misfortune. It is a ſovereign art, a ſovereign myſtery, ſublime and immaculate; clear unto the ſight, virtuous, inexhauſtible, and eaſy to be performed. Thoſe who are infidels to this faith, not finding me, return again into this world, the manſion of death.

This whole world was ſpread abroad by me in my inviſible form. All things are dependent on me, and I am not dependent on them; and all things are not dependent on me[16]. Behold my divine connection! My creative ſpirit is the keeper of all things, not the dependent. Underſtand that all things reſt in me, as the mighty air, which paſſeth every where, reſteth for ever in the ætherial ſpace. At the end of the period *Kalp*[17] all things, O ſon of *Koontee*, return into my primordial ſource, and at the beginning of another *Kalp* I create them all again. I plant myſelf on my own nature, and create, again and again, this aſſemblage of beings, the whole, from the power of *nature*, without power[18]. Thoſe works confine not me, becauſe I am like one who ſitteth aloof unintereſted in thoſe works. By my ſuperviſion *nature* produceth both the moveable and the immoveable. It is from this ſource[19], O *Arjoon*, that the univerſe reſolveth.

The fooliſh, being unacquainted with my ſupreme and divine nature, as lord of all things, deſpiſe me in this human form, truſting to the evil, diabolic, and deceitful

principle

principle within them. They are of vain hope, of vain
endeavours, of vain wifdom, and void of reafon; whilft
men of great minds, trufting to their divine natures, difcover that I am before all things and incorruptible, and
ferve me with their hearts undiverted by other Gods[40].

Men of rigid and laborious lives come before me
humbly bowing down, for ever glorifying my name;
and they are conftantly employed in my fervice; but
others ferve me, worfhipping me, whofe face is turned
on all fides, with the worfhip of wifdom, unitedly, feparately, in various fhapes. I am the facrifice; I am the
worfhip; I am the fpices; I am the invocation; I am
the ceremony to the manes of the anceftors; I am the
provifions; I am the fire, and I am the victim: I am
the father and the mother of this world, the grandfire,
and the preferver. I am the holy one worthy to be
known; the myftic figure *Om;* the *Reek,* the *Sam,* and
Yajoor Veds[41]. I am the journey of the good; the
comforter; the creator; the witnefs; the refting-place;
the afylum, and the friend. I am generation and diffolution, the place where all things are repofited, and the
inexhauftible feed of all nature. I am funfhine, and I
am rain; I now draw in, and now let forth. I am
death and immortality: I am entity and non-entity.

The followers of the three *Veds,* who drink of the
juice of the *Som*[42], being purified of their offences, addrefs me in facrifices, and petition for heaven. Thefe
obtain the regions of *Eendra*[43], the prince of celeftial
beings, in which heaven they feaft upon celeftial food
and divine enjoyments; and when they have partaken
of that fpacious heaven for a while, in proportion to
their virtues, they fink again into this mortal life, as
foon as their ftock of virtue is expended. In this manner thofe, who, longing for the accomplifhment of their
wifhes, follow the religion pointed out by the three
Veds, obtain a tranfient reward. But thofe who, thinking

ing of no other, ferve me alone, I bear the burthen of the devotion of thofe who are thus conftantly engaged in my fervice. They alfo who ferve other Gods with a firm belief, in doing fo, involuntarily worfhip even me. I am he who partaketh of all worfhip, and I am their reward. Becaufe mankind are unacquainted with my nature they fall again from heaven. Thofe who worfhip the *Devatas* go unto the *Devatas;* the worfhippers of the *Peetrees*, or patriarchs, go unto the *Peetrees;* the fervants of the *Bhoots*, or fpirits, go unto the *Bhoots;* and they who worfhip me go unto me.

I accept and enjoy the holy offerings of the humble foul, who in his worfhip prefenteth leaves and flowers, and fruit and water unto me. Whatever thou doeft, O *Arjoon*, whatever thou eateft, whatever thou facrificeft, whatever thou giveft, whatever thou fhalt be zealous about, make each an offering unto me. Thou fhalt thus be delivered with good and evil fruits, and with the bonds of works. Thy mind being joined in the practice of a *Sannyasee*[44], thou fhalt come unto me. I am the fame to all mankind: there is not one who is worthy of my love or hatred. They who ferve me with adoration, I am in them, and they in me. If one, whofe ways are ever fo evil, ferve me alone, he is as refpectable as the juft man; he is altogether well employed; he foon becometh of a virtuous fpirit, and obtaineth eternal happinefs. Recollect, O fon of *Koontee*, that my fervant doth not perifh. Thofe even who may be of the womb of fin; women[45]; the tribes of *Vifya* and *Soodra;* fhall go the fupreme journey, if they take fanctuary with me; how much more my holy fervants the *Brahmans* and the *Rajarfhees*[46]! Confider this world as a finite and joylefs place, and ferve me. Be of my mind, my fervant, my adorer, and bow down before me. Unite thy foul, as it were, unto me, make me thy afylum, and thou fhalt go unto me.

LECTURE

LECTURE X.

OF THE DIVERSITY OF THE DIVINE NATURE.

KREESHNA.

HEAR again, O valiant youth, my fupreme words, which I will fpeak unto thee, who art well pleafed, becaufe I am anxious for thy welfare.

Neither the hofts of *Soors*[47], nor the *Maharfhees*[48], know of my birth; becaufe I am before all the *Devatas* and *Maharfhees*. Whofo, free from folly, knoweth me to be without birth, before all things, and the mighty ruler of the univerfe, he fhall, amongft mortals, be faved with all his tranfgreffions. The various qualities incident to natural beings, fuch as reafon, knowledge, unembarraffed judgment, patience, truth, humility, meeknefs, pleafure and pain; birth and death, fear and courage; mercy, equality, gladnefs, charity, zeal, renown and infamy, all diftinctly come from me. So in former days the feven *Maharfhees* and the four *Manoos*[49] who are of my nature, were born of my mind, of whom are defcended all the inhabitants of the earth. He who knoweth this my diftinction and my connection, according to their principles, is without doubt endued with an unerring devotion. I am the creator of all things, and all things proceed from me. Thofe who are endued with fpiritual wifdom, believe this and worfhip me: their very hearts and minds are in me; they rejoice amongft themfelves, and delight in fpeaking of my name, and teaching one another my doctrine. I gladly infpire thofe, who are conftantly employed in my fervice, with that ufe of reafon, by which they come unto me;

and,

and, in compaffion, I ftand in my own nature, and diffi-
pate the darknefs of their ignorance with the light of
the lamp of wifdom.

ARJOON.

All the *Reefhees*[50], the *Devarfhees*[51], and the prophet
Narad[52], call thee the fupreme *Brahm*; the fupreme
abode; the moft holy; the moft high God; the eternal
Pooroofh, the divine being before all other Gods, without
birth, the mighty Lord! Thus fay *Aseeta, Devala,
Vyas*, and thou thyfelf haft told me fo; and I firmly
believe, O *Kesava*, all thou telleft me. Neither the
Dews nor the *Danoos*[53] are acquainted, O Lord, with
thy appearance. Thou alone, O firft of men[54]! knoweft
thy own fpirit; thou, who art the produ&ion of all
nature, the ruler of all things, the God of Gods, and
the univerfal Lord! Thou art now able to make me
acquainted with thofe divine portions of thyfelf, by
which thou poffeffeft and dwelleft in this world. How
fhall I, although I conftantly think of thee, be able to
know thee? In what particular natures art thou to be
found? Tell me again in full what is thy conne&ion,
and what thy diftin&ion; for I am not yet fatisfied with
drinking of the living water of thy words.

KREESHNA.

Bleffings be upon thee! I will make thee acquainted
with the chief of my divine diftin&ions, as the extent of
my nature is infinite.

I am the foul which ftandeth in the bodies of all
beings. I am the beginning, the middle, and the end
of all things. Amongft the *Adeetyas*[55] I am *Veefhnoo*[56],
and the radiant *Ravee*[57] amongft the ftars; I am *Mareechee*[58] amongft the *Maroots*[59], and *Sasee*[60] amongft the
Nakfhatras[61]; amongft the *Veds* I am the *Sam*[62], and I
am *Vasava*[63] amongft the *Dews*. Amongft the faculties
I am the mind, and amongft animals I am reafon. I

am

am *Sankar*[64] amongſt the *Roodras*[65], and *Veettesa*[66] amongſt the *Yakſhas* and the *Rakſhas*. I am *Pavak*[67] amongſt the *Vasoos*[68] and *Meroo*[69] amongſt the aſpiring mountains. Amongſt teachers know that I am their chief *Vreehaſpatee*[70]; amongſt warriors I am *Skanda*[71]; and amongſt floods I am the ocean. I am *Bhreegoo*[72] amongſt the *Maharſhees*, and I am the monoſyllable[73] amongſt words. I am amongſt worſhips the *Yap*[74] or ſilent worſhip, and amongſt immoveables the mountain *Heemalay*[75]. Of all the trees of the foreſt I am the *Aſwattha*[76], and of all the *Devarſhees* I am *Narad*. I am *Cheetra-rath* amongſt *Gandharvs*[77] and the *Moonee Kapeel* amongſt the ſaints. Know that amongſt horſes I am *Oochiſrava*, who aroſe with the *Amreeta* from out the ocean[78]. Amongſt elephants I am *Iravat*, and the ſovereign amongſt men. Amongſt weapons I am the *Vajra* or thunderbolt, and amongſt cattle the cow *Kama-dhook*[79]. I am the prolific *Kandarp* the God of love; and amongſt ſerpents I am *Vasookee* their chief. I am *Ananta* amongſt the *Nags*[80], and *Varoon*[81] amongſt the inhabitants of the waters. I am *Aryama* amongſt the *Peetrees*, and I am *Yam*[82] amongſt all thoſe who rule. Amongſt the *Dityas* (evil ſpirits) I am *Prablad*[83], and *Kal* (time) amongſt computations. Amongſt beaſts I am the king of beaſts, and *Vinateya*[84] amongſt the feathered tribe. Amongſt purifiers I am *Pavan* the air, and *Ram* amongſt thoſe who carry arms. Amongſt fiſhes I am the *Makar*[85], and amongſt rivers I am *Ganga*[86] the daughter of *Jahnoo*. Of things tranſient I am the beginning, the middle, and the end. Of all ſcience I am the knowledge of the ruling ſpirit, and of all ſpeaking I am the oration. Amongſt letters I am the vowel *a*, and of all compound words I am the *Dwandwa*[87]. I am alſo never-failing time; the preſerver, whoſe face is turned on all ſides. I am all-graſping death; and I am the reſurrection of

thoſe

thofe who are about to be. Amongft fœminines I am fame, fortune, eloquence, memory, underftanding, fortitude, patience. Amongft harmonious meafures I am the *Gayatree*, and amongft *Sams* I am the *Vreebat Sam*. Amongft the months I am the month *Marga-seerfha*[88], and amongft feafons the feafon *Koosoomakara*[89], (spring.) Amongft frauds I am gaming; and of all things glorious I am the glory. I am victory, I am induftry, and I am the effence of all qualities. Of the race of *Vreefhnee* I am the fon of *Vasoodev*[90], and amongft the *Pandoos Arjoon-Dhananjay*. I am *Vyas*[91] amongft the *Moonees*, and amongft the *Bards*[92] I am the prophet *Oofana*[93]. Amongft rulers I am the rod, and amongft thofe who feek for conqueft I am policy. Amongft the fecret I am filence, and amongft the wife I am wifdom. I am, in like manner, O *Arjoon*, that which is the feed of all things in nature; and there is not any thing, whether animate or inanimate, that is without me. My divine diftinctions are without end, and the many which I have mentioned are by way of example. And learn, O *Arjoon*, that every being which is worthy of diftinction and pre-eminence, is the produce of the portion of my glory. But what, O *Arjoon*, haft thou to do with this manifold wifdom? I planted this whole univerfe with a fingle portion and ftood ftill.

LECTURE

LECTURE XI.

DISPLAY OF THE DIVINE NATURE IN THE FORM OF THE UNIVERSE.

ARJOON.

THIS fupreme myftery, diftinguifhed by the name of the *Adhee-atma* or ruling fpirit, which, out of loving-kindnefs, thou haft made known unto me, hath diffipated my ignorance and perplexity. I have heard from thee a full account of the creation and deftruction of all things, and alfo of the mightinefs of thy inexhauftible fpirit. It is even as thou haft defcribed thy-felf, O mighty Lord! I am now, O moft elevated of men, anxious to behold thy divine countenance; wherefore, if thou thinkeft it may be beheld by me, fhew me thy never-failing fpirit.

KREESHNA.

Behold, O *Arjoon*, my million forms divine, of various fpecies, and diverfe fhapes and colours. Behold the *Adeetyas*, and the *Vasoos*, and the *Roodras*, and the *Maroots*, and the twins *Afween* and *Koomar*[94]. Behold things wonderful, never feen before. Behold, in this my body, the whole world animate and inanimate, and all things elfe thou haft a mind to fee. But as thou art unable to fee with thefe thy natural eyes, I will give thee a heavenly eye, with which behold my divine connection.

SANJAY.

The mighty compound and divine being *Haree*, having, O *Raja*, thus fpoken, made evident unto *Arjoon* his fupreme and heavenly form; of many a mouth and eye; many a wondrous fight; many a heavenly orna-

9   ment;

ment; many an up-raifed weapon; adorned with celeftial
robes and chaplets; anointed with heavenly effence;
covered with every marvellous thing; the eternal God,
whofe countenance is turned on every fide! The glory
and amazing splendour of this mighty being may be
likened to the fun rifing at once into the heavens, with
a thoufand times more than ufual brightnefs. The fon
of *Pandoo* then beheld within the body of the God of
Gods, ftanding together, the whole univerfe divided
forth into its vaft variety. He was overwhelmed with
wonder, and every hair was raifed an end. He bowed
down his head before the God, and thus addreffed him
with joined hands.

ARJOON.

I behold, O God! within thy breaft, the *Dews*
affembled, and every fpecific tribe of beings. I fee
Brahma, that Deity fitting on his lotus-throne; all the
Reefhees and heavenly *Ooragas*[95]. I fee thyfelf, on all
fides, of infinite fhape, formed with abundant arms,
and bellies, and mouths, and eyes; but I can neither
difcover thy beginning, thy middle, nor again thy end,
O univerfal Lord, form of the univerfe! I fee thee
with a crown, and armed with club and *Chakra*[96], a mafs
of glory, darting refulgent beams around. I fee thee,
difficult to be feen, fhining on all fides with light im-
meafurable, like the ardent fire or glorious fun. Thou
art the Supreme Being, incorruptible, worthy to be
known! Thou art prime fupporter of the univerfal
orb! Thou art the never-failing and eternal guardian
of religion! Thou art from all beginning, and I efteem
the *Pooroofh*[97]. I fee thee without beginning, without
middle, and without end; of valour infinite; of arms
innumerable; the fun and moon thy eyes; thy mouth
a flaming fire, and the whole world fhining with thy
reflected glory! The fpace between the heavens and
the

the earth is poffeffed by thee alone, and every point around: the three regions of the univerfe, O mighty fpirit! behold the wonders of thy awful countenance with troubled minds. Of the celeftial bands, fome I fee fly to thee for refuge; whilft fome, afraid, with joined hands fing forth thy praife. The *Maharfhees*, holy bands, hail thee, and glorify thy name with adorating praifes. The *Roodras*, the *Adeetyas*, the *Vasoos*, and all thofe beings the world efteemeth good; *Afween* and *Koomar*, the *Maroots* and the *Oofhmapas;* the *Gandharvs* and the *Yakfhas*, with the holy tribes of *Soors*, all ftand gazing on thee, and all alike amazed! The worlds, alike with me, are terrified to behold thy wondrous form gigantic; with many mouths and eyes; with many arms, and legs, and breafts; with many bellies, and with rows of dreadful teeth! Thus as I fee thee, touching the heavens, and fhining with fuch glory; of fuch various hues, with widely-opened mouths, and bright expanded eyes, I am difturbed within me; my refolution faileth me, O *Veefhnoo!* and I find no reft! Having beholden thy dreadful teeth, and gazed on thy countenance, emblem of Time's laft fire, I know not which way I turn! I find no peace! Have mercy then, O God of Gods! thou manfion of the univerfe! The fons of *Dhreetarafhtra*, now, with all thofe rulers of the land, *Bheefhma*, *Dron*, the fon of *Soot*, and even the fronts of our army, feem to be precipitating themfelves haftily into thy mouths, difcovering fuch frightful rows of teeth! whilft fome appear to ftick between thy teeth with their bodies forely mangled. As the rapid ftreams of full-flowing rivers roll on to meet the ocean's bed; even fo thefe heroes of the human race rufh on towards thy flaming mouths. As troops of infects, with increafing fpeed, feek their own deftrution in the flaming fire; even fo thefe people, with fwelling fury,

feek

feek their own deftruction. Thou involveft and fwalloweft them altogether, even unto the laft, with thy flaming mouths; whilft the whole world is filled with thy glory, as thy awful beams, O *Veefhnoo*, fhine forth on all fides! Reverence be unto thee, thou moft exalted! Deign to make known unto me who is this God of awful figure! I am anxious to learn thy fource, and ignorant of what thy prefence here portendeth.

KREESHNA.

I am Time, the deftroyer of mankind, matured, come hither to feize at once all thefe who ftand before us. Except thyfelf⁹⁸ not one of all thefe warriors, deftined againft us in thefe numerous ranks, fhall live. Wherefore, arife! feek honor and renown! defeat the foe, and enjoy the full-grown kingdom! They are already, as it were, deftroyed by me. Be thou alone the immediate agent⁹⁹. Be not difturbed! Kill *Dron*, and *Bheefhma*, and *Jayadrath*, and *Karna*, and all the other heroes of the war already killed by me. Fight! and thou fhalt defeat thy rivals in the field.

SANJAY.

When the trembling *Arjoon* heard thefe words from the mouth of *Kreefhna*, he faluted him with joined hands, and addreffed him in broken accents, and bowed down terrified before him.

ARJOON.

Ottreefheekes! the univerfe rejoiceth because of thy renown, and is filled with zeal for thy fervice. The evil fpirits are terrified and flee on all fides; whilft the holy tribes bow down in adoration before thee. And wherefore fhould they not, O mighty Being! bow down before thee, who, greater than *Brahma*, art the prime Creator! eternal God of Gods! the world's manfion! Thou art the incorruptible Being, diftinct from all things tranfient! Thou art before all Gods, the ancient *Pooroofh,*

Pooroofh, and the fupreme fupporter of the univerfe! Thou knoweft all things, and art worthy to be known; thou art the fupreme manfion, and by thee, O infinite form! the univerfe was fpread abroad. Thou art *Vayoo* the God of the wind, *Agnee* the God of fire, *Varoon* the God of oceans, *Sasanka* the moon, *Prajapatee* the God of nations, and *Prapeetamaha* the mighty anceftor. Reverence! Reverence be unto thee a thoufand times repeated! Again and again Reverence! Reverence be unto thee! Reverence be unto thee before and behind! Reverence be unto thee on all fides, O thou who art all in all! Infinite is thy power and they glory! Thou includeft all things, wherefore thou art all things! Having regarded thee as my friend, I forcibly called thee *Kreefhna*, *Yadava*, Friend! but alas! I was ignorant of this thy greatnefs, becaufe I was blinded by my affection and prefumption. Thou haft, at times, alfo in fport been treated ill by me; in thy recreations, in thy bed, on thy chair, and at thy meals; in private and in public; for which, O Being inconceivable! I humbly crave thy forgivenefs.

Thou art the father of all things animate and inanimate; thou art the fage inftructor of the whole, worthy to be adored! There is none like unto thee; where then, in the three worlds, is there one above thee? Wherefore I bow down; and, with my body proftrate upon the ground, crave thy mercy, Lord! worthy to be adored; for thou fhouldft bear with me, even as a father with his fon, a friend with his friend, a lover with his beloved. I am well pleafed with having beheld things before never feen; yet my mind is overwhelmed with awful fear. Have mercy, then, O heavenly Lord! O manfion of the univerfe! and fhew me thy celeftial form. I wish to behold thee with the diadem on thy head, and thy hands armed with club and *Chakra*; affume then, O God

of

of a thoufand arms, image of the univerfe! thy four-armed form [100].

KREESHNA.

Well pleafed, O *Arjoon*, I have fhewn thee, by my divine power, this my fupreme form the univerfe, in all its glory, infinite and eternal, which was never feen by any one except thyfelf; for no one, O valiant *Kooroo!* in the three worlds, except thyfelf, can fuch a fight of me obtain; nor by the *Veds*, nor facrifices, nor profound ftudy; nor by charitable gifts, nor by deeds, nor by the moft fevere mortification of the flefh. Having beholden my form, thus awful, be not difturbed, nor let thy faculties be confounded. When thou art relieved from fears, and thy mind is reftored to peace, then behold this my wondrous form again.

SANJAY.

The fon of *Vasoodev* having thus fpoken unto *Arjoon*, fhewed him again his natural form; and having re-affumed his milder fhape, he prefently affwaged the fears of affrighted *Arjoon*.

ARJOON.

Having beheld thy placid human fhape, I am again collected; my mind is no more difturbed, and I am once more returned to my natural ftate.

KREESHNA.

Thou haft beholden this my marvellous fhape, fo very difficult to be feen, which even the *Dews* are con-ftantly anxious to behold. But I am not to be feen, as thou haft feen me, even by the affiftance of the *Veds*, by mortifications, by facrifices, by charitable gifts; but I am to be feen, to be known in truth, and to be obtained by means of that worfhip which is offered up to me alone; and he goeth unto me whofe works are done for me; who efteemeth me fupreme; who is my fervant only; who hath abandoned all confequences, and who liveth amongft all men without hatred.

LECTURE

LECTURE XII.

OF SERVING THE DEITY IN HIS VISIBLE AND INVISIBLE FORMS.

ARJOON.

OF thofe thy fervants who are always thus employed, which know their duty beft? thofe who worfhip thee as thou now art; or thofe who ferve thee in thy invifible and incorruptible nature?

KREESHNA.

Thofe who having placed their minds in me, ferve me with conftant zeal, and are endued with fteady faith, are efteemed the beft devoted. They too who, delighting in the welfare of all nature, ferve me in my incorruptible, ineffable, and invifible form; omniprefent, incomprehenfible, ftanding on high fixed and immoveable, with fubdued paffions and underftandings, the fame in all things, fhall alfo come unto me. Thofe whofe minds are attached to my invifible nature have the greater labour to encounter; becaufe an invifible path is difficult to be found by corporeal beings. They alfo who, preferring me, leave all works for me, and, free from the worfhip of all others, contemplate and ferve me alone, I prefently raife them up from the ocean of this region of mortality, whofe minds are thus attached to me. Place then thy heart on me, and penetrate me with thy underftanding, and thou fhalt, without doubt, hereafter enter unto me. But if thou fhouldft be unable, at once, ftedfaftly to fix thy mind on me, endeavour to find me by means of conftant practice. If after practice thou art ftill unable, follow me in my wórks fupreme; for by performing works for me, thou fhalt attain perfection.

But

But fhouldft thou find thyfelf unequal to this tafk, put thy truft in me alone, be of humble fpirit, and forsake the fruit of every action. Knowledge is better than practice, meditation is diftinguifhed from knowledge, forfaking the fruit of action from meditation, for happinefs hereafter is derived from fuch forfaking.

He my fervant is dear unto me, who is free from enmity, the friend of all nature, merciful, exempt from pride and felfifhnefs, the fame in pain and pleafure, patient of wrongs, contented, conftantly devout, of fubdued paffions, and firm refolves, and whose mind and underftanding are fixed on me alone. He alfo is my beloved of whom mankind are not afraid, and who of mankind is not afraid ; and who is free from the influence of joy, impatience, and the dread of harm. He my fervant is dear unto me who is unexpecting, just and pure, impartial, free from diftraction of mind, and who hath forfaken every enterprize. He alfo is worthy of my love, who neither rejoiceth nor findeth fault ; who neither lamenteth nor coveteth, and, being my fervant, hath forfaken both good and evil fortune. He alfo is my beloved fervant, who is the fame in friendfhip and in hatred, in honor and in difhonor, in cold and in heat, in pain and pleafure ; who is unfolicitous about the event of things ; to whom praife and blame are as one ; who is of little fpeech, and pleafed with whatever cometh to pafs ; who owneth no particular home, and who is of a fteady mind. They who feek this *Amreeta*[101] of religion even as I have faid, and ferve me faithfully before all others, are, moreover, my deareft friends.

LECTURE

LECTURE XIII.

EXPLANATION OF THE TERMS KSHE-TRA AND KSHETRA-GNA.

ARJOON.

I NOW am anxious to be informed, O *Kesoo!* what is *Prakreetee*, who is *Pooroosh;* what is meant by the words *Kshetra* and *Kshetra-gna,* and what by *Gnan* and *Gneya.*

KREESHNA.

Learn that by the word *Kshetra* is implied this body, and that he who is acquainted with it is called *Kshetra-gna.* · Know that I am that *Kshetra-gna* in every mortal frame. The knowledge of the *Kshetra* and the *Kshetra-gna* is by me esteemed *Gnan* or wisdom.

Now hear what that *Kshetra* or body is, what it resembleth, what are its different parts, what it proceedeth from, who he is who knoweth it, and what are its productions. Each hath been manifoldly sung by the *Ree-shees* in various measures, and in verses containing divine precepts, including arguments and proofs.

This *Kshetra* or body, then, is made up of the five *Mahabhoot* (elements), *Ahankar* (self-consciousness), *Bood-hee* (understanding), *Avyaktam* (invisible spirit), the eleven *Eendreeya* (organs), and the five *Eendreeya-gochar* (faculties of the five senses); with *Eecha* and *Dwesha* (love and hatred), *Sookh* and *Dookh* (pleasure and pain), *Chetana* (sensibility), and *Dhreetee* (firmness).

Thus have I made known unto thee what that *Kshetra* or body is, and what are its component parts.

Gnan, or wisdom, is freedom from self-esteem, hypocrisy and injury; patience, rectitude, respect for masters

10   and

and teachers, chaſtity, ſteadineſs, ſelf-conſtraint, diſaffec-
tion for the objeƈts of the ſenſes, freedom from pride,
and a conſtant attention[102] to birth, death, decay, ſick-
neſs, pain and defeƈts; exemption from attachments
and affeƈtion[103] for children, wife, and home; a conſtant
evenneſs of temper upon the arrival of every event,
whether longed for or not; a conſtant and invariable
worſhip paid to me alone; worſhipping in a private
place, and a diſlike to the ſociety of man; a conſtant
ſtudy of the ſuperior ſpirit[104]; and the inſpeƈtion of the
advantage to be derived from a knowledge of the *Tattwa*
or firſt principle.

This is what is diſtinguiſhed by the name of *Gnan*, or
wiſdom. *Agnan*, or ignorance, is the reverſe of this.

I will now tell thee what is *Gnea*, or the object of wiſdom, from underſtanding which thou wilt enjoy immortality. It is that which hath no beginning, and is
ſupreme, even *Brahm*, who can neither be called *Sat* (ens)
nor *Aſat* (non ens)[105]. It is all hands and feet; it is
all faces, heads, and eyes; and, all ear, it ſitteth in the
midſt of the world poſſeſſing the vaſt whole. Itſelf
exempt from every organ, it is the refleƈted light of
every faculty of the organs. Unattached, it containeth
all things; and without quality it partaketh of every
quality. It is the inſide and the outſide, and it is the
moveable and immoveable of all nature. From the
minuteneſs of its parts it is inconceivable. It ſtandeth
at a diſtance, yet is it preſent. It is undivided, yet in
all things it ſtandeth divided. It is the ruler of all
things: it is that which now deſtroyeth, and now produceth. It is the light of lights, and it is declared to
be free from darkneſs. It is wiſdom, that which is the
objeƈt of wiſdom, and that which is to be obtained by
wiſdom; and it preſideth in every breaſt.

Thus hath been deſcribed together what is *Kſhetra* or
body

body, what is *Gnan* or wifdom, and what is *Gneya* or the objeft of wifdom. He my fervant who thus conceiveth me obtaineth my nature.

Learn that both *Prakreetee* and *Pooroofh* are without beginning. Know alfo that the various component parts of matter and their qualities are co-exiftent with *Prakreetee*.

Prakreetee is that principle which operateth in the agency of the inftrumental caufe of aftion.

Pooroofh is that *Hetoo* or principle which operateth in the fenfation of pain and pleafure. The *Pooroofh* refideth in the *Prakreetee*, and partaketh of thofe qualities which proceed from the *Prakreetee*. The confequences arifing from thofe qualities, are the caufe which operateth in the birth of the *Pooroofh*[106], and determineth whether it fhall be in a good or evil body. *Pooroofh* is that fuperior being, who is called *Mahefwar*, the great God, the moft high fpirit, who in this body is the obferver, the direftor, the proteftor, the partaker.

He who conceiveth the *Pooroofh* and the *Prakreetee*, together with the *Goon* or qualities, to be even fo as I have defcribed them, whatever mode of life he may lead, he is not again fubjeft to mortal birth.

Some men, by meditation, behold, with the mind, the fpirit within themfelves; others, according to the difcipline of the *Sankhya* (contemplative doftrines), and the difcipline which is called *Karma-yog* (praftical doctrines); others again, who are not acquainted with this, but have heard it from others, attend to it. But even thefe, who aft but from the report of others, pafs beyond the gulf of death.

Know, O chief of the race of *Bharat*, that every thing which is produced in nature, whether animate or inanimate, is produced from the union of *Kfhetra* and *Kfhetragna*, matter and fpirit. He who beholdeth the Supreme Being

Being alike in all things, whilft corrupting, itfelf uncorrupting; and conceiving that God in all things is the fame, doth not of himfelf injure his own foul, goeth the journey of immortality. He who beholdeth all his actions performed by *Prakreetee,* nature, at the fame time perceiveth that the *Atma* or foul is inactive in them. When he beholdeth all the different fpecies in nature comprehended in one alone, and fo from it fpread forth into their vaft variety, he then conceiveth *Brahm,* the Supreme Being. This fupreme fpirit and incorruptible Being, even when it is in the body, neither acteth, nor is it affected, becaufe its nature is without beginning and without quality. As the all-moving *Akas,* or ether, from the minutenefs of its parts, paffeth every where unaffected, even fo the omniprefent fpirit remaineth in the body unaffected. As a fingle fun illuminateth the whole world, even fo doth the fpirit enlighten every body. They who, with the eye of wifdom, perceive the body and the fpirit to be thus diftinct, and that there is a final releafe from the animal nature, go to the Supreme.

LECTURE

LECTURE XIV.

OF THE THREE GOON OR QUALITIES.

KREESHNA.

I WILL now reveal unto thee a moſt ſublime knowledge, ſuperior to all others, which having learnt,
all the *Moonees* have paſſed from it to ſupreme perfection.
They take ſanctuary under this wiſdom, and being arrived to that virtue which is ſimilar to my own, they
are not diſturbed on the day of the confuſion of all
things, nor born again on their renovation.

The great *Brahm* is my womb. In it I place my
fœtus; and from it is the production of all nature. The
great *Brahm* is the womb of all thoſe various forms
which are conceived in every natural womb, and I am
the father who ſoweth the ſeed.

There are three *Goon* or qualities ariſing from *Prakreetee* or nature: *Satwa* truth, *Raja* paſſion, and *Tama*
darkneſs; and each of them confineth the incorruptible
ſpirit in the body. The *Satwa-Goon*, becauſe of its
purity, is clear and free from defect, and intwineth the
ſoul with ſweet and pleaſant conſequences, and the fruit
of wiſdom. The *Raja-Goon* is of a paſſionate nature,
ariſing from the effects of worldly thirſt, and impriſoneth
the ſoul with the conſequences produced from action.
The *Tama-Goon* is the offspring of ignorance, and the
confounder of all the faculties of the mind; and it impriſoneth the ſoul with intoxication, ſloth, and idleneſs.
The *Satwa-Goon* prevaileth in felicity, the *Raja* in action,
and the *Tama*, having poſſeſſed the ſoul, prevaileth in
intoxication. When the *Tama* and the *Raja* have been

overcome,

overcome, then the *Satwa* appeareth; when the *Raja* and the *Satwa*, the *Tama*; and when the *Tama* and the *Satwa*, the *Raja*. When *Gnan*, or wifdom, fhall become evident in this body at all its gates, then fhall it be known that the *Satwa-Goon* is prevalent within. The love of gain, induftry, and the commencement of works; intemperance, and inordinate defire, are produced from the prevalency of the *Raja-Goon*; whilft the tokens of the *Tama-Goon* are gloominefs, idlenefs, fottifhnefs, and diftraction of thought. When the body is diffolved whilft the *Satwa-Goon* prevaileth, the foul proceedeth to the regions of those immaculate beings who are acquainted with the Moft High. When the body findeth diffolution whilft the *Raja-Goon* is predominate, the foul is born again amongft thofe who are attached to the fruits of their actions. So, in like manner, fhould the body be diffolved whilft the *Tama-Goon* is prevalent, the fpirit is conceived again in the wombs of irrational beings. The fruit of good works is called pure and holy; the fruit of the *Raja-Goon* is pain; and the fruit of the *Tama-Goon* is ignorance. From the *Satwa* is produced wifdom, from the *Raja* covetoufnefs, and from the *Tama* madnefs, diftraction, and ignorance. Thofe of the *Satwa-Goon* mount on high, thofe of the *Raja* ftay in the middle, whilft thofe abject followers of the *Tama-Goon* fink below.

When he who beholdeth perceiveth no other agent than thefe qualities, and difcovereth that there is a being fuperior to them, he at length findeth my nature; and when the foul hath furpaffed thefe three qualities, which are co-exiftent with the body, it is delivered from birth and death, old-age and pain, and drinketh of the water of immortality.

ARJOON.

By what tokens is it known that a man hath furpaffed
thefe

thefe three qualities? What is his practice? What are the means by which he overcometh them.

KREESHNA.

He, O fon of *Pandoo*, who defpifeth not the light of wifdom, the attention to worldly things, and the diftraction of thought when they come upon him, nor longeth for them when they disappear; who, like one who is of no party, fitteth unagitated by the three qualities; who, whilft the qualities are prefent, ftandeth ftill and moveth not; who is felf-dependent and the fame in eafe and pain, and to whom iron, ftone, and gold are as one; firm alike in love and diflike, and the fame whether praifed or blamed; the fame in honor and difgrace; the fame on the part of the friend and the foe, and who forfaketh all enterprize; such a one hath furmounted the influence of the qualities. And he, my fervant, who ferveth me alone with due attention, having overcome the influence of the qualities, is formed to be abforbed in *Brahm*, the Supreme. I am the emblem of the immortal, and of the incorruptible; of the eternal, of juftice, and of endlefs blifs.

LECTURE

LECTURE XV.

OF POOROOSHOTTAMA.

KREESHNA.

THE incorruptible being is likened unto the tree *Af-wattha*, whofe root is above and whofe branches are below, and whofe leaves are the *Veds*. He who knoweth that, is acquainted with the *Veds*. Its branches growing from the three *Goon* or qualities, whofe leffer fhoots are the objects of the organs of fenfe, fpread forth fome high and fome low. The roots which are fpread abroad below, in the regions of mankind, are reftrained by action. Its form is not to be found here, neither its beginning, nor its end, nor its likenefs. When a man hath cut down this *Afwattha*, whofe root is fo firmly fixed, with the ftrong ax of difintereft, from that time that place is to be fought from whence there is no return for thofe who find it; and I make manifeft that firft *Pooroofh* from whom is produced the ancient progreffion of all things.

Thofe who are free from pride and ignorance, have prevailed over thofe faults which arife from the confe-quences of action, have their minds conftantly employed in watching over and reftraining the inordinate defires, and are freed from contrary caufes, whofe confequences bring both pleafure and pain, are no longer confounded in their minds, and afcend to that place which endureth for ever. Neither the fun, nor the moon, nor the fire enlighteneth that place from whence there is no return, and which is the fupreme manfion of my abode.

It is even a portion of myfelf that in this animal world is the univerfal fpirit of all things. It draweth together

together the five organs and the mind, which is the
fixth, that it may obtain a body, and that it may leave
it again; and *Eefwar*, having taken them under his
charge, accompanieth them from his own abode as the
breeze the fragrance from the flower. He prefideth over
the organs of hearing, feeing, feeling, tafting, and fmelling, together with the mind, and attendeth to their objects. The foolifh fee it not, attended by the *Goon* or
qualities, in expiring, in being, or in enjoying; but
thofe who are endued with the eye of wifdom behold
it. Thofe alfo who induftrioufly apply their minds in
meditation may perceive it planted in their own breafts,
whilft thofe of unformed minds and weak judgments,
labouring, find it not.

Know that the light which proceedeth from the fun
and illuminateth the whole world, and the light which
is in the moon, and in the fire, are mine. I pervade all
things in nature, and guard them with my beams. I
am the moon, whofe nature it is to give the quality of
tafte and relifh, and to cherifh the herbs and plants of
the field. I am the fire refiding in the bodies of all
things which have life, where, joined with the two fpirits
which are called *Pran* and *Opan* [107], I digeft the food
which they eat, which is of four kinds [108]. I penetrate
into the hearts of all men; and from me proceed memory, knowledge, and the lofs of both. I am to be
known by all the *Veds* or books of divine knowledge:
I am he who formed the *Vedant* [109], and I am he who
knoweth the *Veds*.

There are two kinds of *Pooroofh* in the world, the one
corruptible, the other incorruptible. The corruptible
Pooroofh is the body of all things in nature; the incorruptible is called *Koothafta*, or he who ftandeth on the
pinnacle [110]. There is another *Pooroofh* [111] moft high, the
Paramatma, or fupreme foul, who inhabiteth the three
regions

regions of the world, even the incorruptible *Eeſwar*. Becauſe I am above corruption, ſo alſo am I ſuperior to incorruption; wherefore in this world, and in the *Veds*, I am called *Poorooſhottama*. The man of a ſound judgment, who conceiveth me thus to be the *Poorooſhottama*, knoweth all things, and ſerveth me in every principle.

Thus, O *Arjoon*, have I made known unto thee this moſt myſterious *Saſtra*[112]; and he who underſtandeth it ſhall be a wiſe man, and the performer of all that is fit to be done.

LECTURE

LECTURE XVI.

OF GOOD AND EVIL DESTINY.

KREESHNA.

THE man who is born with divine deſtiny is endued
with the following qualities : exemption from fear,
a purity of heart, a conſtant attention to the diſcipline
of his underſtanding; charity, ſelf-reſtraint, religion,
ſtudy, penance, rectitude, freedom from doing wrong,
veracity, freedom from anger, reſignation, temperance,
freedom from ſlander, univerſal compaſſion, exemption
from the deſire of ſlaughter, mildneſs, modeſty, diſcre-
tion, dignity, patience, fortitude, chaſtity, unrevenge-
fulneſs, and a freedom from vain-glory : whilſt thoſe who
come into life under the influence of the evil destiny
are diſtinguiſhed by hypocriſy, pride, preſumption, anger,
harſhneſs of ſpeech, and ignorance. The divine deſtiny
is for *Mokſh,* or eternal abſorption in the divine nature;
and the evil deſtiny confineth the ſoul to mortal birth.
Fear not, *Arjoon,* for thou art born with the divine
deſtiny before thee. Thus there are two kinds of deſtiny prevailing in the world. The nature of the good
deſtiny hath been fully explained. Hear what is the
nature of the evil.

Thoſe who are born under the influence of the evil
deſtiny know not what it is to proceed in virtue, or recede from vice; nor is purity, veracity, or the practice
of morality to be found in them. They ſay the world
is without beginning, and without end, and without an
Eeſwar; that all things are conceived by the junction
of the ſexes; and that love is the only cauſe. Theſe
loſt ſouls, and men of little underſtandings, having fixed
upon

upon this vifion, are born of dreadful and inhuman
deeds for the deftruction of the world. They truft to
their carnal appetites, which are hard to be fatisfied; are
hypocrites, and overwhelmed with madnefs and intoxication. Becaufe of their folly they adopt falfe doctrines,
and continue to live the life of impurity. They abide
by their inconceivable opinions, even unto the day of
confufion, and determine within their own minds that
the gratification of the fenfual appetites is the fupreme
good. Faft bound by the hundred cords of hope, and
placing all their truft in luft and anger, they feek by injuftice the accumulation of wealth, for the gratification
of their inordinate defires. "This, to-day, hath been
"acquired by me. I fhall obtain this object of my
"heart. This wealth I have, and this fhall I have alfo.
"This foe have I already flain, and others will I forth-
"with vanquifh. I am *Eefwar*, and I enjoy; I am
"confummate, I am powerful, and I am happy; I am
"rich, and I am endued with precedence amongft men;
"and where is there another like unto me? I will make
"prefents at the feafts and be merry." In this manner
do thofe ignorant men talk, whofe minds are thus gone
aftray. Confounded with various thoughts and defigns,
they are entangled in the net of folly; and being firmly
attached to the gratification of their lufts, they fink at
length into the *Narak* of impurity. Being felf-con-
ceited, ftubborn, and ever in purfuit of wealth and pride,
they worfhip with the name of worfhip and hypocrify,
and not according to divine ordination; and, placing
all their truft in pride, power, oftentation, luft, and
anger, they are overwhelmed with calumny and detrac-
tion, and hate me in themfelves and others: wherefore
I caft down upon the earth thofe furious abject wretches,
thofe evil beings who thus defpife me, into the wombs
of evil fpirits and unclean beafts. Being doomed to
the

the wombs of *Afoors* from birth to birth, at length not finding me, they go unto the moſt infernal regions. There are these three paſſages to *Narak* (or the infernal regions) ; luſt, anger, and avarice, which are the deſtroyers of the foul ; wherefore a man ſhould avoid them ; for, being freed from theſe gates of ſin, which ariſe from the influence of the *Tama-Goon*, he advanceth his own happineſs ; and at length he goeth the journey of the Moſt High. He who abandoneth the dictates of the *Saſtra* to follow the dictates of his luſts, attaineth neither perfection, happineſs, nor the regions of the Moſt High. Wherefore, O *Arjoon*, having made thyſelf acquainted with the precepts of the *Saſtra*, in the eſtabliſhment of what is fit and unfit to be done, thou ſhouldſt perform thoſe works which are declared by the commandments of the *Saſtra*.

LECTURE

LECTURE XVII.

OF FAITH DIVIDED INTO THREE SPECIES.

ARJOON.

WHAT is the guide of thofe men, who, although they neglect the precepts of the *Saftra*, yet, worfhip with faith? Is it the *Satwa*, the *Raja* or the *Tama-Goon*?

KREESHNA.

The faith of mortals is of three kinds, and is produced from the conftitution. It is denominated after the three *Goon*, *Satwakee*, *Rajasee*, or *Tamasee*. Hear what thefe are. The faith of every one is a copy of that which is produced from the *Satwa-Goon*. The mortal *Pooroofh* being formed with faith, of whatever nature he may be, with that kind of faith is he endüed. Thofe who are of the difpofition which arifeth from the *Satwa-Goon* worfhip the *Dews*; thofe of the *Raja-Goon* the *Yakfhas*, and the *Rakfhas*; and thofe of the *Tama-Goon* worfhip the departed fpirits and the tribe of *Bhoots*. Thofe men who perform fevere mortifications of the flesh, not authorized by the *Saftra*, are poffeffed of hypocrify and pride, and overwhelmed with luft, paffion, and tyrannic ftrength. Thofe fools torment the fpirit that is in the body, and myfelf alfo who am in them. Know what are the refolutions of thofe who are born under the influence of the evil fpirit.

There are three kinds of food which are dear unto all men. Worfhip, zeal[1], and charity are each of them alfo divided into three fpecies. Hear what are their diftinctions.

The

The food that is dear unto thofe of the *Satwa-Goon*
is fuch as increases their length of days, their power and
their ftrength, and keeps them free from ficknefs, happy
and contented. It is pleafing to the palate, nourifhing,
permanent, and congenial to the body. It is neither
too bitter, too four, too falt, too hot, too pungent, too
aftringent, nor too inflammable. The food that is coveted by thofe of the *Raja-Goon* giveth nothing but pain
and mifery: and the delight of thofe in whom the
Tama-Goon prevaileth, is fuch as was dreffed the day
before, and is out of feafon, hath loft its tafte, and is
grown putrid; the leavings of others, and all things
that are impure.

That worfhip which is directed by divine precept, and
is performed without the defire of reward, as neceffary to
be done, and with an attentive mind, is of the *Satwa-Goon*.

The worfhip which is performed with a view to the
fruit, and with hypocrify, is of the *Tama-Goon*.

The worfhip which is performed without regard to
the precepts of the law, without the diftribution of bread,
without the ufual invocations, without gifts to the *Brahmans* at the conclufion, and without faith, is of the
Raja-Goon.

Refpect to the *Dews*, to *Brahmans*, mafters, and learned
men; chaftity, rectitude, the worfhip of the Deity, and
a freedom from injury, are called *bodily zeal*.

Gentlenefs, juftnefs, kindnefs, and benignity of fpeech,
and attention to one's particular ftudies, are called *verbal
zeal*.

Content of mind, mildnefs of temper, devotion, reftraint of the paffions, and a purity of foul, are called
mental zeal.

This threefold zeal being warmed with fupreme faith,
and performed by men who long not for the fruit of
action, is of the *Satwa-Goon*.

The

The zeal which is fhewn by hypocrify, for the fake of the reputation of fanctity, honor, and refpect, is faid to be of the *Raja-Goon ;* and it is inconftant and uncertain.

The zeal which is exhibited with felf-torture, by the fool, without examination, or for the purpofe of injuring another, is of the *Tama-Goon.*

That charity which is beftowed by the difinterefted, becaufe it is proper to be given, in due place and feafon, and to proper objects, is of the *Satwa-Goon.*

That which is given in expectation of a return, or for the fake of the fruit of the action, and with reluctancy, is of the *Raja-Goon.*

That which is given out of place and feafon, and to unworthy objects, and, at the fame time, ungracioufly and fcornfully, is pronounced to be of the *Tama-Goon.*

ॐ *Ōm,* तत् *Tat,* and सत् *Sat,* are the three myftic characters ufed to denote the Deity.

By him in the beginning were appointed the *Brahmans,* the *Veds,* and religion : hence the facrificial, charitable, and zealous ceremonies of the expounders of the word of God, as they are ordained by the law, conftantly proceed after they have pronounced *Om !*

Tat having been pronounced by thofe who long for immortality, without any inclination for a temporary reward of their actions, then are performed the ceremonies of worfhip and zeal, and the various deeds of charity.

The word *Sat* is ufed for qualities which are true, and for qualities that are holy. The word *Sat* is alfo applied to deeds which are praifeworthy. Attention in worfhip, zeal, and deeds of charity, are alfo called *Sat.* Deeds which are performed for *Tat* are alfo to be efteemed *Sat.*

Whatever is performed without faith, whether it be facrifices, deeds of charity, or mortifications of the flefh, is called *Asat ;* and is not for this world or that which is above.

LECTURE

LECTURE XVIII.

OF FORSAKING THE FRUITS OF ACTION FOR OBTAINING ETERNAL SALVATION.

ARJOON.

I WISH much to comprehend the principle of *Sannyas*, and alfo of *Tyag*, each feparately.

KREESHNA.

The bards conceive[114] that the word *Sannyas* implieth the forfaking of all actions which are defirable; and they call *Tyag*, the forfaking of the fruits of every action. Certain philofophers have declared that works are as much to be avoided as crimes; whilft others fay that deeds of worfhip, mortifications, and charity fhould not be forfaken. Hear what is my decree upon the term *Tyag*.

Tyag, or forfaking, is pronounced to be of three natures. But deeds of worfhip, mortification, and charity are not to be forfaken : they are proper to be performed. Sacrifices, charity, and mortifications are purifiers of the philofopher. It is my ultimate opinion and decree, that fuch works are abfolutely to be performed, with a forfaking of their confequences and the profpect of their fruits. . The retirement from works, which are appointed to be performed, is improper.

The forfaking of them through folly and diftraction of mind, arifeth from the influence of the *Tama-Goon*.

The forfaking of a work becaufe it is painful, and from the dread of bodily affliction, arifeth from the *Raja-Goon;* and he who thus leaveth undone what he ought to do, fhall not obtain the fruit of forfaking.

The work which is performed becaufe it is appointed
and

and efteemed neceffary to be done, and with a forfaking
of the confequences and the hope of a reward, is, with
fuch a forfaking, declared to be of the *Satwa-Goon*.

The man who is poffeffed of the *Satwa-Goon* is thus a
Tyagee, or one who forfaketh the fruit of action. He is
of a found judgment, and exempt from all doubt; he
complaineth not in adverfity, nor exulteth in the fuccefs
of his undertakings.

No corporeal being is able totally to refrain from
works. He is properly denominated a *Tyagee* who is a
forfaker of the fruit of action.

The fruit of action is threefold: that which is coveted,
that which is not coveted, and that which is neither one
nor the other. Thofe who do not abandon works obtain a final releafe; not thofe who withdraw from action,
and are denominated *Sannyasees*.

Learn, O *Arjoon*, that for the accomplifhment of
every work five agents [115] are neceffary, as is further declared in the *Sankhya* and *Vedant-Saftras*:—attention
and fupervifion, the actor, the implements of various
forts, diftinct and manifold contrivances, and laftly the
favor of Providence. The work which a man under-
taketh, either with his body, his fpeech, or his mind,
whether it be lawful or unlawful, hath thefe five agents
engaged in the performance. He then who after this,
becaufe of the imperfection of his judgment, beholdeth
no other agent than himfelf, is an evil-thinker and feeth
not at all. He who hath no pride in his difpofition,
and whofe judgment is not affected, although he fhould
deftroy a whole world, neither killeth, nor is he bound
thereby [116].

In the direction of a work are three things: *Gnan*,
Gneya, and *Pareegnata* [117]. The accomplifhment of a
work is alfo threefold: the implement, the action, and
the agent. The *Gnan*, the action, and the agent are
each

each diftinguished by the influence of the three *Goon*.
Hear in what manner they are declared to be after the.
order of the three *Goon*.

That *Gnan*, or wifdom, by which one principle alone
is feen prevalent in all nature, incorruptible and infinite
in all things finite; is of the *Satwa-Goon*.

That *Gnan*, or wifdom, is of the *Raja-Goon*, by which
a man believeth that there are various and manifold
principles prevailing in the natural world of created
beings.

That *Gnan*, or wifdom which is mean, interefted in
one fingle objeƈt alone as if it were the whole, without
any juft motive or defign, and without principle or
profit, is pronounced to be of the *Tama-Goon*.

The aƈtion which is appointed by divine precept, is
performed free from the thought of its confequences and
without paffion or defpite, by one who hath no regard
for the fruit thereof, is of the *Satwa-Goon*.

The aƈtion which is performed by one who is fond
of the gratification of his lufts, or by the proud and
felfifh, and is attended with unremitted pains, is of the
Raja-Goon.

The aƈtion which is undertaken through ignorance
and folly, and without any forefight of its fatal and in-
jurious confequence, is pronounced to be of the *Tama-
Goon*.

The agent who is regardlefs of the confequences, is
free from pride and arrogance, is endued with fortitude
and refolution, and is unaffeƈted whether his work fucceed or not, is faid to be of the *Satwa-Goon*.

That agent is pronounced to be of the *Raja-Goon* who
is a flave to his paffions, who longeth for the fruit of
aƈtion, who is avaricious, of a cruel difpofition, of impure principles, and a flave to joy and grief.

The agent who is unattentive, indifcreet, ftubborn,
diffembling,

diffembling, mifchievous, indolent, melancholy, and dilatory, is of the *Tama-Goon*.

Hear alfo what are the threefold divfions of underftanding and firmnefs, according to the influence of the three *Goon*, which are about to be explained to thee diftinctly and without referve.

The underftanding which can determine what it is to proceed in a bufinefs, and what it is to recede; what is neceffary and what is unneceffary; what is fear and what is not; what is liberty and what is confinement, is of the *Satwa-Goon*.

The underftanding which doth .not conceive juftice and injuftice; what is proper and what is improper; as they truly are, is of the *Raja-Goon*.

The underftanding which, being overwhelmed in darknefs, miftaketh injuftice for juftice, and all things contrary to their true intent and meaning, is of the *Tama-Goon*.

That fteady firmnefs, with which a man, by devotion, reftraineth every action of the mind and organs, is of the *Satwa-Goon*.

That interefted firmness by which a man, from views of profit, perfifteth in the duties of his calling, in the gratification of his lufts, and the acquifition of wealth, is declared to be of the *Raja-Goon*.

That ftubborn firmnefs, by which a man of low capacity departeth not from floth, fear, grief, melancholy, and intoxication, is of the *Tama-Goon*.

Now hear what is the threefold divifion of pleafure.

That pleafure which a man enjoyeth from his labour, and wherein he findeth the end of his pains; and that which, in the beginning, is as poifon, and in the end as the water of life, is declared to be of the *Satwa-Goon*, and to arife from the confent of the underftanding.

That pleafure which arifeth from the conjunction of the

the organs with their objects, which in the beginning is as fweet as the water of life, and in the end as a poifon, is of the *Raja-Goon.*

That pleafure which in the beginning and the end tendeth to ftupify the foul, and arifeth from drowfinefs, idlenefs, and intoxication, is pronounced to be of the *Tama-Goon.*

There is not any thing either in heaven or earth, or amongft the hofts of heaven, which is free from the influence of thefe three *Goon* or qualities, which arife from the firft principles of nature.

The refpective duties of the four tribes of *Brahman*[118], *Kfhetree*[119], *Vifya,* and *Soodra*[120], are alfo determined by the qualities which are in their conftitutions.

The natural duty of the *Brahman* is peace, felf-reftraint, zeal, purity, patience, rectitude, wifdom, learning, and theology.

The natural duties of the *Kfhetree* are bravery, glory, fortitude, rectitude, not to flee from the field, generofity, and princely conduct.

The natural duty of the *Vifya* is to cultivate the land, tend the cattle, and buy and fell.

The natural duty of a *Soodra* is fervitude.

A man being contented with his own particular lot and duty obtaineth perfection. Hear how that perfection is to be accomplifhed.

The man who maketh an offering of his own works to that being from whom the principles of all beings proceed, and by whom the whole univerfe was fpread forth, by that means obtaineth perfection.

The duties of a man's own particular calling, although not free from faults, is far preferable to the duty of another, let it be ever fo well purfued. A man by following the duties which are appointed by his birth, doeth no wrong. A man's own calling, with all its faults,
ought

ought not to be forſaken. Every undertaking is involved in its faults, as the fire in its smoke. A diſintereſted mind and conquered ſpirit, who, in all things, is free from inordinate deſires, obtaineth a perfection unconnected with works, by that reſignation and retirement which is called *Sannyas;* and having attained that perfection, learn from me, in brief, in what manner he obtaineth *Brahm,* and what is the foundation of wiſdom.

A man being endued with a purified underſtanding, having humbled his ſpirit by reſolution, and abandoned the objects of the organs; who hath freed himſelf from paſſion and diſlike; who worſhippeth with diſcrimination, eateth with moderation, and is humble of ſpeech, of body, and of mind; who preferreth the devotion of meditation, and who conſtantly placeth his confidence in diſpaſſion; who is freed from oſtentation, tyrannic ſtrength, vain-glory, luſt, anger, and avarice; and who is exempt from ſelfiſhneſs, and in all things temperate, is formed for being *Brahm.* And thus being as *Brahm,* his mind is at eaſe, and he neither longeth nor lamenteth. He is the ſame in all things, and obtaineth my ſupreme aſſiſtance; and by my divine aid he knoweth, fundamentally, who I am, and what is the extent of my exiſtence; and having thus diſcovered who I am, he at length is abſorbed in my nature.

A man alſo being engaged in every work, if he put his truſt in me alone, ſhall, by my divine pleaſure, obtain the eternal and incorruptible manſions of my abode.

With thy heart place all thy works on me; prefer me to all things elſe; depend upon the uſe of thy underſtanding, and think conſtantly of me; for by doing ſo thou ſhalt, by my divine favor, ſurmount every difficulty which ſurroundeth thee. But if, through pride, thou wilt not liſten unto my words, thou ſhalt undoubtedly be loſt. From a confidence in thy own ſelf-ſufficiency

ficiency thou mayft think that thou wilt not fight. Such is a fallacious determination, for the principles of thy nature will impel thee. Being confined to action by the duties of thy natural calling, thou wilt involuntarily do that from neceffity, which thou wanteft, through ignorance, to avoid.

Eefwar refideth in the breaft of every mortal being, revolving with his fupernatural power all things which are mounted upon, the univerfal wheel of time. Take fanctuary then, upon all occafions, with him alone, O offspring of *Bharat;* for by his divine pleafure thou fhalt obtain fupreme happinefs and an eternal abode.

Thus have I made known unto thee a knowledge which is a fuperior myftery. Ponder it well in thy mind, and then act as it feemeth beft unto thee.

Attend now to thefe my fupreme and moft myfterious words, which I will now for thy good reveal unto thee, becaufe thou art dearly beloved of me. Be of my mind, be my fervant, offer unto me alone and bow down humbly before me, and thou fhalt verily come unto me; for I approve thee, and thou art dear unto me. For-fake every other religion, and fly to me alone. Grieve not then, for I will deliver thee from all thy tranfgreffions.

This is never to be revealed by thee to any one who hath not fubjected his body by devotion, who is not my fervant, who is not anxious to learn; nor unto him who defpifeth me.

He who fhall teach this fupreme myftery unto my fervant, directing his fervice unto me, fhall undoubtedly go unto me; and there fhall not be one amongft man-kind who doeth me a greater kindnefs; nor fhall there be in all the earth one more dear unto me.

He alfo who fhall read thefe our religious dialogues, by him I may be fought with the devotion of wifdom. This is my refolve.

The

The man too who may only hear it without doubt, and with due faith, may alfo be faved, and obtain the regions of happinefs provided for thofe whofe deeds are virtuous.

Hath what I have been fpeaking, O *Arjoon*, been heard with thy mind fixed to one point? Is the diftraction of thought, which arofe from thy ignorance, removed?

Arjoon.

By thy divine favor, my confufion of mind is loft, and I have found underftanding. I am now fixed in my principles, and am freed from all doubt; and I will henceforth act according to thy words.

Sanjay.

In this manner have I been an ear-witnefs of the aftonifhing and miraculous converfation that hath paffed between the fon of *Vasoodev*, and the magnanimous fon of *Pandoo*; and I was enabled to hear this fupreme and miraculous doctrine, even as revealed from the mouth of *Kreefhna* himfelf, who is the God of religion, by the favor of *Vyas*[111]. As, O mighty Prince! I recollect again and again this holy and wonderful dialogue of *Kreefhna* and *Arjoon*, I continue more and more to rejoice; and as I recall to my memory the more than miraculous form of *Haree*[112], my aftonifhment is great, and I marvel and rejoice again and again! Wherever *Kreefhna* the God of devotion may be, wherever *Arjoon* the mighty bowman may be, there too, without doubt, are fortune, riches, victory, and good conduct. This is my firm belief.

THE END OF THE GEETA.

NOTES.

N O T E S

TO THE

G E E T A.

13

N O T E S.

24 1 THE *ancient chief.*—*Bheeſhma*, brother of *Veecheetra-veerya*, grandfather of the *Kooroos* and the *Pandoos*.

— 2 *Shell.*—The conch or chank.

— 3 *Kreeſhna.*—An incarnation of the Deity.

— 4 *Arjoon.*—The third son of *Pandoo*, and the favorite of *Kreeſhna*.

26 l. 3 *Gandeev my bow.*—The gift of *Varoon* the God of the Ocean.

— 5 *Hell.*—In the original *Nark*. The infernal regions, ſuppoſed to be ſituated at the bottom of the earth, where thoſe whoſe virtues are leſs than their vices are doomed to dwell for a period proportioned to their crimes, after which they riſe again to inhabit the bodies of unclean beaſts.

27 6 *Forefathers, &c.*—The Hindoos are enjoined by the *Veds* to offer a cake, which is called *Peenda*, to the ghoſts of their anceſtors, as far back as the third generation. This ceremony is performed on the day of the new moon in every month. The offering of water is in like manner commanded to be performed daily, and this ceremony is called *Tarpan*, to ſatisfy, appeaſe.—The ſouls of ſuch men as have left children to continue their generation, are ſuppoſed to be tranſported, immediately upon quitting their bodies, into a certain region called *Peetree-log*, where they may continue in proportion to their former

former virtues, provided thefe ceremonies be not
negleded; otherwife they are precipitated into *Nark*,
and doomed to be born again in the bodies of unclean beafts; and until, by repeated regenerations,
all their fins are done away, and they attain fuch a
degree of perfection as will entitle them to what is
called *Mooktee*, eternal falvation, by which is underftood a releafe from future tranfmigration, and an
abforption in the nature of the Godhead, who is
called *Brahm*. Thefe ceremonies, which are called
Sradh, were not unknown to the Greeks and Ro-
mans, and are ftill pradifed by the followers of
Mahommed.

28   7   *Contrary to duty.*—Contrary to the duty of a foldier.

29   8   *By the dictates of my duty.*—The duty of a foldier in
oppofition to the dictates of the general moral duties.

—   9   *The wife men.*—*Pandeets*, or expounders of the law;
or in a more general fenfe, fuch as by meditation
have attained that degree of perfection which is
called *Gnan*, or infpired wifdom.

31   10   *The bonds of action.*—The Hindoos believe that every
action of the body, whether good or evil, confineth
the foul to mortal birth; and that an eternal releafe,
which they call *Mooktee*, is only to be attained by a
total neglect of all fublunary things, or, which is the
fame thing according to the doctrine of *Kreefhna*,
the abandonment of all hopes of the reward of our
actions; for fuch reward, they fay, can only be a
fhort enjoyment of a place in heaven, which they
call *Swarg;* because no man can, merely by his
actions, attain perfection, owing to the mixture of
good and evil which is implanted in his conftitution.

32   11   *The objects of the Veds are of a threefold nature.*—The
commentators do not agree with refpect to the fignification of this paffage; but, as the *Veds* teach
three diftinct fyftems of religion, it is probable that
it refers to this circumftance.

—   12   *Yog.*—There is no word in the *Sanfkreet* language that
will bear fo many interpretations as this. Its firft
fignification is *junction* or *union.* It is alfo ufed for
bodily

bodily or mental application; but in this work it is generally ufed as a theological term, to exprefs the application of the mind in fpiritual things, and the performance of religious ceremonies. The word *Yogee*, a devout man, is one of its derivatives. If the word *devotion* be confined to the performance of religious duties, and a contemplation of the Deity, it will generally ferve to exprefs the fenfe of the original; as will *devout* and *devoted* for its derivatives.

32 ¹³ *Wifdom.*—Wherever the word *wifdom* is ufed in this Tranflation, is to be understood *infpired wifdom*, or a knowledge of the Divine Nature. The original word is *Gnan*, or as it is written *Jnan*.

33 ¹⁴ *Folly.*—In the original *Moha*, which fignifies an embaraffment of the faculties, arifing from the attendant qualities of the principles of organized matter.

35 ¹⁵ *The practice of deeds.*—The performance of religious ceremonies and moral duties, called *Karma-Yog*.

36 ¹⁶ *Brahma.*—The Deity in his creative quality.

— ¹⁷ *Hath no occafion.*—Hath no occafion to perform the ceremonial parts of religion.

37 ¹⁸ *Attained perfection.*—That degree of perfection which is neceffary to falvation.

38 ¹⁹ *Defire.*—The will, as prefiding over the organs, the heart and the underftanding.

39 ²⁰ *The refolution.*—In this place refolution means the power of diftinguifhing the truth of a propofition: the underftanding.

— ²¹ *He.*—The foul, or univerfal fpirit, of which the vital foul is fuppofed to be a portion.

41 ²² *Worfhip the Devatas.*—The word *Devata* is fynonymous with *Dev*, *Dew*, or *Deb*, as it is fometimes pronounced. The Angels, or fubordinate celeftial beings; all the attributes of the Deity; and every thing in Heaven and Earth which has been perfonified by the imagination of the Poets.

43 ²³ *And where, O Arjoon, is there another?*—*fit for him* is underftood. The fentence would perhaps read better in this form: " He who neglecteth the duties of " life

Page. No.

             "life is not for this world, much lefs for that which
             "is above." But the other tranflation is literally
             correct.

43   14 *In me.*—In the Deity, who is the univerfal fpirit.

—   15 *Have no power to confine.*—Have no power to confine
             the foul to mortal birth.

45   26 *In the nine-gate city of its abode.*—The body, as fur-
             nifhed with nine paffages for the action of the
             faculties : the eyes, nofe, mouth, &c.

—   27 *The powers nor the deeds of mankind.*—To underftand
             this, and many fimilar paffages, it is neceffary to be
             apprized that the Hindoos believe that all our actions,
             whether good or evil, arife from the inherent quali-
             ties of the principles of our conftitution.

50   28 *The man, &c.*—i. e. That the defire of becoming a
             devout man is equal to the ftudy of the *Veds.*

52   29 *Of a vital nature.*—The vital foul.

— l. 20 *Learn that thefe two.*—Matter and fpirit.

53   30 *Satwa, Raja, Tama.*—*Truth, paffion, darkness;* or, as
             the words are fometimes ufed, *white, red, black.*

—   31 *The wifhers after wealth.*—Such as pray for worldly
             endowments.

—   32 *And are governed by their own principles.*—By the three
             ruling qualities already explained.

55   33 *Adhee-atma, &c.*— As *Kreefhna's* anfwer to the feveral
             queftions of *Arjoon* has fomething myfterious in it, I
             will endeavour to render it more comprehenfible :

             Adhee-atma—literally fignifies *the over-ruling fpirit*, by
             which is implied the divine nature.

             Karma—fignifies *action*, whereby is to be underftood
             his creative quality.

             Adhee-bhoot—fignifies *he who ruleth over created beings :*
             the power of the Deity to deftroy.

             Adhee-diva—literally means *fuperior to fate ;* and is ex-
             plained by the word *Pooroofh*, which, in vulgar lan-
             guage, means no more than man ; but in this work
             it is a term in theology ufed to exprefs the vital foul,
             or portion of the univerfal fpirit of *Brahm* inhabiting
             a body. So by the word *Maha-Pooroofh* is implied
             the Deity as the *primordial source.* Thefe terms are
                                         ufed

ufed in a metaphyfical work called *Patanjal*, wherein God is reprefented under the figure of *Maha-Poo-rooſh*, the great man or prime progenitor; in conjunction with *Prakreetee*, nature or firſt principle, under the emblem of a female engendering the world with his *Maya* or fupernatural power.

56   34   *Om!*—This myſtic emblem of the Deity is forbidden to be pronounced but in filence. It is a fyllable formed of the letters ℞ *a*, ℥ *oo*, which in compofition coalefce, and make ℥ *O*, and the nafal confonant ℞ *m*. The firſt letter ſtands for the Creator, the fecond for the Preferver, and the third for the Deſtroyer.

—   35   *A thousand revolutions of the Yoogs.*—Is equal to 4320,-000,000 years. An ingenious mathematician, who is now in India, fuppofes that thefe *Yoogs* are nothing more than aſtronomical periods formed from the coincidence of certain cycles, of which thofe of the preceſſion of the equinoxes and the moon are two. The word *Yoog*, which fignifies a *juncture* or *joining*, gives good grounds for fuch an hypothefis.

58   36   *And all things are not dependent on me.*—This ambiguity is removed by the following fimile of the air in the æther.

—   37   *Kalp.*—The fame as the day of *Brahma*, a thoufand revolutions of the *Yoogs*. The word literally fignifies *formation*.

—   38   *The whole, from the power of nature, without power.*—This paffage is agreeable to the doctrine of the influence of the three *Goon*, or qualities, over all our actions.

—   39   *It is from this fource.*—Becaufe of the fupervifion of the Supreme Being.

59   40   *Other Gods.*—Wherever the word *Gods* is ufed in this Tranflation, the fubordinate fupernatural beings are implied.

—   41   *Veds.*—The word *Ved* fignifies *learning*. The facred volumes of the Hindoos, of which there are four, fuppofed to have been revealed from the four mouths of *Brahma*. It is remarkable that *Kreeſhna* mentions

tions only the three firſt; it may therefore be pre-
ſumed that no more exiſted in his time.

59   42 *Som.*—is the name of a creeper, the juice of which
is commanded to be drank at the concluſion of a
ſacrifice, by the perſon for whom and at whoſe
expence it is performed, and by the *Brahmans* who
officiate at the altar.

—   43 *Eendra*—is a perſonification of the viſible heavens, or
the power of the Almighty over the elements. He
is the ſprinkler of the rain, the roller of the thunder,
and director of the winds. He is repreſented with
a thouſand eyes, graſping the thunderbolt.

60   44 *Sannyasee*—one who totally forſaketh all worldly actions;
but *Kreeſhna*, in order to unite the various religious
opinions which prevailed in thoſe days, confines the
word *Sannyas* to a forſaking of the hope of reward.

—   45 *Women.*—In the *Veds* it is declared, that the ſouls of
women, and of the inferior tribes, are doomed to .
tranſmigration till they can be regenerated in the
body of a *Brahman*.

—   46 *Rajarſhees*—from *Raja* and *Reeſhee*, Prince and Saint.

61   47 *Soors.*—Good angels.

—   48 *Maharſhees.*—Great *ſaints*, of whom there are reckoned
ſeven, who were at the creation produced from the
mind of *Brahma*.

—   49 *Manoos.*—Four other beings produced at the creation
from the mind of *Brahma*.

62   50 *Reeſhees.*—Saints.

—   51 *Devarſhees.*—Deified ſaints.

—   52 *Narad.*—One of the *Devarſhees*, and a great Prophet,
who is ſuppoſed to be ſtill wandering about the
world. *Nara* ſignifies a thread or clew, a precept;
and *Da* Giver.—Wherever he appears he is conſtantly employed in giving good counſel.

—   53 *Danoos.*—Evil ſpirits, or fallen angels, the offsprings
of *Danoo* (fem).

—   54 *O firſt of men !*—*Arjoon* makes uſe of this expreſſion as
addreſſing the Deity in human ſhape.

—   55 *Adeetyas.*—The offsprings of *Adeetee* (f.) (that may not
be cut off.) There are reckoned twelve, and are
nothing

nothing more than emblems of the fun for each month of the year. Their names are *Varoon, Soorya, Vedang, Bhanoo, Eendra, Ravee, Gabbaftee, Yam, Swarna-reta, Deevakar, Meetra, Veefhnoo.*

62   56 *Veefhnoo.*—He who filleth or poffeffeth all fpace. One of the twelve funs, and the name of the Deity in his preferving quality.

— 57 *Ravee.*—The rifer—one of the names of the fun.

— 58 *Mareechee.*—One of the eight points of the heavens.

— 59 *Maroots.*—The winds.

— 60 *Sasee.*—The moon.

— 61 *Nakfhatras.*—Difpellers of darknefs. The 18 con-ftellations through which the moon paffes in its monthly courfe. Conftellations in general.

— 62 *Sam.*—The firft of the four books of the *Veds,* com-pofed to be chanted or fung.

— 63 *Vasava.*—One of the names of *Eendra.*

63   64 *Sankar.*—One of the names of *Seev,* or Fate.

— 65 *Roodras.*—Eleven diftinctions of *Seev,* or Fate.

— 66 *Veettesa.*—The God of riches, otherwife called *Koover.* He is faid to prefide over the regions of the north, and to be the chief of the *Yakfhas* and the *Rakfhas,* two fpecies of good and evil Genii.

— 67 *Pavak.*—The God of fire. He is fuppofed to prefide over the foutheaft quarter.

— 68 *Vasoos.*—Eight of the firft created Beings of *Brahma.*

— 69 *Meroo.*—The north pole of the terreftrial globe, fabled by the poets to be the higheft mountain in the world. It is fometimes, by way of pre-eminence, called *Soo-meroo.* It is remarkable that the word *Meroo* fignifies a centre or axis.

— 70 *Vreehafpatee.*—The preceptor of the *Devs* or *Dews,* the planet Jupiter and *Dies Jovis.*

— 71 *Skanda.*—Otherwife called *Karteek,* the general of the celeftial armies.

— 72 *Bhreegoo.*—One of the firft created beings produced from the mind of *Brahma.*

— 73 *The monofyllable.*—The myftic word or monofyllable ॐ *Om!* already explained.

— 74 *Yap.*—A filent repetition of the name of God.

63   75 *Heemalay.*

AN EPISODE FROM THE *MAHABHARAT*,
Book I. Chap. 15.

"THERE is a fair and ftately mountain, and its name is *Meroo*, a moft exalted mafs of glory, reflecting the funny rays from the fplendid furface of its gilded horns. It is cloathed in gold, and is the refpected haunt of *Dews* and *Gandharvs*. It is inconceivable, and not to be encompaffed by finful man ; and it is guarded by dreadful ferpents. Many celeftial medicinal plants adorn its fides, and it ftands, piercing the heavens with its afpiring fummit, a mighty hill inacceffible even by the human mind ! It is adorned with trees and pleafant ftreams, and refoundeth with the delightful fongs of various birds.

The

The *Soors*, and all the glorious hofts of heaven, having afcended to the fummit of this lofty mountain, fparkling with precious gems, and for eternal ages raifed, were fitting, in folemn fynod, meditating the difcovery of the *Amreeta*, or water of immortality. The *Dew Narayan* being alfo there, fpoke unto *Brahma*, whilft the *Soors* were thus confulting together, and faid, " Let the ocean, " as a pot of milk, be churned by the united labour of the *Soors* " and *Asoors;* and when the mighty waters have been ftirred up, " the *Amreeta* fhall be found. Let them colleƌ together every " medicinal herb, and every precious thing, and let them ftir the " ocean, and they fhall difcover the *Amreeta*."

There is alfo another mighty mountain whofe name is *Mandar*, and its rocky fummits are like towering clouds. It is cloathed in a net of the entangled tendrils of the twining creeper, and refoundeth with the harmony of various birds. Innumerable favage beafts infeft its borders, and it is the refpeƌed haunt of *Keennars*, *Dews*, and *Apsars*. It ftandeth eleven thoufand *Yojan* above the earth, and eleven thoufand more below its furface.

As the united bands of *Dews* were unable to remove this mountain, they went before *Veefhnoo*, who was fitting with *Brahma*, and addreffed them in thefe words : " Exert, O mafters, " your moft fuperior wifdom to remove the mountain *Mandar*, " and employ your utmoft power for our good."

Veefhnoo and *Brahma* having faid, " It fhall be according to " your wifh," he with the lotus eye direƌed the King of Serpents to appear ; and *Ananta* arofe, and was inftruƌed in that work by *Brahma*, and commanded by *Narayan* to perform it. Then *Ananta*, by his power, took up that king of mountains, together with all its forefts and every inhabitant thereof ; and the *Soors* accompanied him into the prefence of the Ocean, whom they addreffed, faying, " We will ftir up thy waters to obtain the " *Amreeta*." And the Lord of the waters replied—" Let me " alfo have a fhare, feeing I am to bear the violent agitations that " will be caufed by the whirling of the mountain." Then the *Soors* and the *Asoors* fpoke unto *Koorma-raj*, the King of the Tortoifes, upon the ftrand of the ocean, and faid—" My Lord is able " to be the fupporter of this mountain." The Tortoife replied, " Be it fo :" and it was placed upon his back.

So the mountain being fet upon the back of the Tortoife, *Eendra* began to whirl it about as it were a machine. The mountain *Mandar* ferved as a churn, and the ferpent *Vasookee* for

the

the rope; and thus in former days did the *Dews*, the *Asoors*, and the *Danoos*, begin to ftir up the waters of the ocean for the difcovery of the *Amreeta*.

The mighty *Asoors* were employed on the fide of the ferpent's head, whilft all the *Soors* affembled about his tail. *Ananta*, that fovereign *Dew*, ftood near *Narayan*.

They now pull forth the ferpent's head repeatedly, and as often let it go; whilft there iffued from his mouth, thus violently drawing to and fro by the *Soors* and *Asoors*, a continual ftream of fire, and fmoke, and wind; which afcending in thick clouds replete with lightning, it began to rain down upon the heavenly bands, who were already fatigued with their labour; whilft a fhower of flowers was fhaken from the top of the mountain, covering the heads of all, both *Soors* and *Asoors*. In the mean time the roaring of the ocean, whilft violently agitated with the whirling of the mountain *Mandar* by the *Soors* and *Asoors*, was like the bellowing of a mighty cloud.—Thoufands of the various productions of the waters were torn to pieces by the mountain, and confounded with the briny flood; and every fpecific being of the deep, and all the inhabitants of the great abyfs which is below the earth, were annihilated; whilft, from the violent agitation of the mountain, the foreft trees were dafhed againft each other, and precipitated from its utmoft height, with all the birds thereon; from whofe violent confrication a raging fire was produced, involving the whole mountain with fmoke and flame, as with a dark blue cloud, and the lightning's vivid flafh. The lion and the retreating elephant are overtaken by the devouring flames, and every vital being, and every fpecific thing, are confumed in the general conflagration.

The raging flames, thus fpreading deftruction on all fides, were at length quenched by a fhower of cloud-borne water poured down by the immortal *Eendra*. And now a heterogeneous ftream of the concocted juices of various trees and plants ran down into the briny flood.

It was from this milk-like ftream of juices produced from those trees and plants, and a mixture of melted gold, that the *Soors* obtained their immortality.

The waters of the ocean now being affimilated with those juices, were converted into milk, and from that milk a kind of butter was prefently produced; when the heavenly bands went again into the prefence of *Brahma*, the granter of boons, and

addreffed

addreffed him, faying—" Except *Narayan*, every other *Soor* and
" *Asoor* is fatigued with his labour, and ftill the *Amreeta* doth
" not appear ; wherefore the churning of the ocean is at a ftand."
Then *Brahma* faid unto *Narayan*—" Endue them with recruited
" ftrength, for thou art their fupport." And *Narayan* anfwered
and faid—" I will give frefh vigour to fuch as co-operate in the
" work. Let *Mandar* be whirled about, and the bed of the
" ocean be kept fteady."

When they heard the words of *Narayan*, they all returned
again to the work, and began to ftir about with great force that
butter of the ocean ; when there prefently arofe from out the
troubled deep—firft the moon, with a pleafing countenance,
fhining with ten thoufand beams of gentle light ; next followed
Sree, the Goddefs of fortune, whofe feat is the white lily of the
waters ; then *Soora-Devee*, the Goddefs of wine, and the white
horfe called *Oochifrava*. And after thefe there was produced,
from the unctuous mafs, the jewel *Kowftoobh*, that glorious fparkling gem worn by *Narayan* on his breaft ; fo *Pareejat*, the tree
of plenty, and *Soorabhee*, the cow that granted every heart's
defire.

The moon, *Soora-Devee*, the Goddefs *Sree*, and the horfe as
fwift as thought, inftantly marched away towards the *Dews*, keeping in the path of the fun.

Then the *Dew Dhanwantaree*, in human fhape, came forth,
holding in his hand a white veffel filled with the immortal juice
Amreeta. When the *Asoors* beheld thefe wondrous things appear,
they raifed their tumultuous voices for the *Amreeta*, and each of
them clamoroufly exclaimed—" This of right is mine !"

In the mean time *Iravat*, a mighty elephant, arofe, now kept
by the God of thunder ; and as they continued to churn the
ocean more than enough, that deadly poifon iffued from its bed,
burning like a raging fire, whofe dreadful fumes in a moment
fpread throughout the world, confounding the three regions of the
univerfe with its mortal ftench ; until *Seev*, at the word of
Brahma, fwallowed the fatal drug to fave mankind ; which re-
maining in the throat of that fovereign *Dew* of magic form, from
that time he hath been called *Neel-Kant*, becaufe his throat was
ftained blue.

When the *Asoors* beheld this miraculous deed, they became
defperate, and the *Amreeta* and the Goddefs *Sree* became the
fource of endlefs hatred.

Then

Then *Narayan* aſſumed the character and perſon of *Moheenee Maya*, the power of inchantment, in a female form of wonderful beauty, and ſtood before the *Aſoors*; whoſe minds being faſcinated by her preſence, and deprived of reaſon, they ſeized the *Amreeta*, and gave it unto her.

The *Aſoors* now cloath themſelves in coſtly armour, and, ſeizing their various weapons, ruſh on together to attack the *Soors*. In the mean time *Narayan*, in the female form, having obtained the *Amreeta* from the hands of their leader, the hoſts of *Soors*, during the tumult and confuſion of the *Aſoors*, drank of the living water.

And it ſo fell out, that whilſt the *Soors* were quenching their thirſt for immortality, *Rahoo*, an *Aſoor*, aſſumed the form of a *Soor*, and began to drink alſo. And the water had but reached his throat, when the ſun and moon, in friendſhip to the *Soors*, diſcovered the deceit; and inſtantly *Narayan* cut off his head, as he was drinking, with his ſplendid weapon *Chakra*. And the gigantic head of the *Aſoor*, emblem of a mountain's ſummit, being thus ſeparated from his body by the *Chakra's* edge, bounded into the heavens with a dreadful cry, whilſt his ponderous trunk fell cleaving the ground aſunder, and ſhaking the whole earth unto its foundation, with all its iſlands, rocks, and foreſts. And from that time the head of *Rahoo* reſolved an eternal enmity, and continueth, even unto this day, at times to ſeize upon the ſun and moon.

Now *Narayan*, having quitted the female figure he had aſſumed, began to diſturb the *Aſoors* with ſundry celeſtial weapons; and from that inſtant a dreadful battle was commenced, on the ocean's briny ſtrand, between the *Aſoors* and the *Soors*. Innumerable ſharp and miſſile weapons were hurled, and thouſands of piercing darts and battle-axes fell on all ſides. The *Aſoors* vomit blood from the wounds of the *Chakra*, and fall upon the ground pierced by the ſword, the ſpear, and ſpiked club.—Heads, glittering with poliſhed gold, divided by the *Pattees'* blade, drop inceſſantly; and mangled bodies, wallowing in their gore, lay like fragments of mighty rocks ſparkling with gems and precious ores. Millions of ſighs and groans ariſe on every ſide; and the ſun is overcaſt with blood, as they claſh their arms, and wound each other with their dreadful inſtruments of deſtruction.

Now the battle's fought with the iron-ſpiked club, and, as they cloſe, with clenched fiſt; and the din of war aſcendeth to the
heavens!

heavens! They cry—"Purfue! ftrike! fell to the ground!" fo that a horrid and tumultuous noife is heard on all fides.

In the midft of this dreadful hurry and confufion of the fight, *Nar* and *Narayan* entered the field together. *Narayan* beholding a celeftial bow in the hand of *Nar*, it reminded him of his *Chakra*, the deftroyer of the *Asoors*. The faithful weapon, by name *Soodarsan*, ready at the mind's call, flew down from heaven with direct and refulgent fpeed, beautiful, yet terrible to behold. And being arrived, glowing like the facrificial flame, and fpreading terror around, *Narayan*, with his right arm formed like the elephantine trunk, hurled forth the ponderous orb, the fpeedy meffenger, and glorious ruin of hoftile towns; who, raging like the final all-deftroying fire, fhot bounding with defolating force, killing thoufands of the *Asoors* in his rapid flight, burning and involving, like the lambent flame, and cutting down all that would oppofe him. Anon he climbeth the heavens, and now again darteth into the field like a *Peesach* to feaft in blood.

Now the dauntlefs *Asoors* ftrive, with repeated ftrength, to crufh the *Soors* with rocks and mountains, which, hurled in vaft numbers into the heavens, appeared like fcattered clouds, and fell, with all the trees thereon, in millions of fear-exciting torrents, ftriking violently againft each other with a mighty noife; and in their fall the earth, with all its fields and forefts, is driven from its foundation: they thunder furioufly at each other as they roll along the field, and fpend their ftrength in mutual conflict.

Now *Nar*, feeing the *Soors* overwhelmed with fear, filled up the path to heaven with fhowers of golden-headed arrows, and fplit the mountain fummits with his unerring fhafts; and the *Asoors*, finding themselves again fore preffed by the *Soors*, precipitately flee: fome rufh headlong into the briny waters of the ocean, and others hide themfelves within the bowels of the earth.

The rage of the glorious *Chakra*, *Soodarsan*, which for a while burnt like the oil-fed fire, now grew cool, and he retired into the heavens from whence he came. And the *Soors* having obtained the victory, the mountain *Mandar* was carried back to its former ftation with great refpect; whilft the waters alfo retired, filling the firmament and the heavens with their dreadful roarings.

The *Soors* guarded the *Amreeta* with great care, and rejoiced exceedingly becaufe of their fuccefs; and *Eendra*, with all his immortal bands, gave the water of life unto *Narayan*, to keep it for their ufe."

63   79   *Kama-dhook.*

Page. No.

63   79 *Kama-dhook.*—One of the names of the Cow of Plenty, produced in churning the ocean.

—   80 *Ananta amongst the Nags.*—The *Nags* are ferpents fabled with many heads. *Ananta* fignifies *eternal,* and may be an emblem of eternity. There are fome very wonderful ftories told of thefe ferpents in the original from which thefe Dialogues are taken.

—   81 *Varoon.*—The God of the Ocean.

—   82 *Yam.*—The judge of hell.

—   83 *Prahlad.*—An evil fpirit who was converted by *Kreefhna.*

—   84 *Vinateya.*—A bird fabled to be of wonderful fize, and the vehicle of *Veefhnoo,* the Deity in his preferving quality, and who is otherwife called *Garoor,*

—   85 *Makar.*—A fifh reprefented with a long fnout fomething like the probofcis of an elephant ; and the fign Capricornus.

—   86 *Ganga.*—The Ganges. When the river was firft conducted from its fource, by a Prince whofe name was *Bhageerath,* towards the ocean, it fo fell out that *Jahnoo* was at his devotions at the mouth of the *Mahanadee,* at a place now called *Navobgunge.*—The Goddefs in paffing fwept away the utenfils for his ablutions, which fo enraged him, that he drank up her ftream ; but after a while his anger was appeafed, and he let her efcape from an incifion made in his thigh ; and from this circumftance of her fecond birth, fhe was afterwards called *Jahnavee,* or the offspring of *Jahnoo.*

—   87 *Dwandwa.*—A term in grammar, ufed where many nouns are put together without a copulative, and the cafe fubjoined to the laft only, which is a mode of compofition much admired by the Poets.

64   88 *Marga-seerfha.*—The month beginning with the middle of October, when the periodical rains have fubfided, and the exceffive heats are abated.

—   89 *Koosoomakara.*—The feafon of flowers, otherwife called *Vasant.* The two months between the middle of March and May.—The Hindoos divide the year into fix *Reetoo,* or feafons, of two months each, which are thus denominated :

Seesar.

Seesar.—Dewy feason.

Heemant.—Cold feason.

Vasant.—Mild (spring).

Greeshma.—Hot feason.

Varsa.—Rainy feason.

Sarat.—Breaking (up of the rains).

64   90   *Vasoodev.*—The father of *Kreeshna* in his incarnation.

—   91   *Vyas.*—The reputed author or compiler of the *Mahabharat.*

—   92   *Bards.*—The Poets of India, like the Bards of Britain, were revered as Saints and Prophets.

—   93   *Oosana.*—Otherwife called *Sookra*, efteemed the preceptor of the evil fpirits ; the planet Venus, and *dies Veneris.*

65   94   *Afween and Koomar.*—Reputed the twin offsprings of the Sun, and phyficians of the Gods.

66   95   *Ooragas.*—*Who crawl upon their breafts :*—ferpents.

—   96   *Chakra.*—A kind of *difcus* with a fharp edge, hurled in battle from the point of the fore-finger, for which there is a hole in the centre.—See the ftory of the churning of the ocean, p. 106.

—   97   *Pooroosh.*—Already explained.

68   98   *Except thyfelf.*—*Thyfelf* fhould include his brothers, who were alfo faved.

—   99   *The immediate agent.*—The inftrument to execute the decree of Fate.

70   100   *Thy four-armed form.*—In which the Deity is ufually reprefented in his incarnations, the images of which *Arjoon* had been accuftomed to behold without emotion.

72   101   *Amreeta.*—The water of immortality, the *Ambrofia* of the Hindoo Gods.—See the ftory of churning the ocean, p. 106.

74   102   *And a conftant attention to birth,* &c.—To look upon them as evils.

—   103   *Exemption from attachments and affection,* &c.—i. e. That no attachments or affections fhould draw a man from the exercife of his devotion ; or that all worldly cares muft be abandoned for the attainment of that wifdom which is to free the foul from future birth.

—   104   *The fuperior fpirit.*—God, the univerfal foul.

74   105   *Sat*

74 105 *Sat (ens) nor Asat (non ens).*—The oppofite meanings of
thefe two words render this paffage peculiarly mys-
terious; and even the commentators differ about
their true fignification. The moft rational interpretation of them is, that the Deity in his works is a
fubftance, or a material Being, and in his effence
immaterial; but as he is but one, he cannot pofitively be denominated either one or the other.

75 106 *Are the caufe which operateth in the birth of the Pooroofh,
&c.*—That is, The influence of the three *Goon*, or
qualities, over the human mind, not only determines
the future birth of the foul, but into what rank of
beings it fhall tranfmigrate; for to tranfmigrate it is
doomed, until it hath attained a degree of wifdom
more powerful than the influence of thofe qualities.

81 107 *Pran and Opan.*—The breathing fpirit, and the fpirit
which acteth in the bowels to expel the fæces.

— 108 *Which is of four kinds.*—Either to be mafticated with
the teeth, lapped in with the tongue, fucked in by
the lips, or imbibed by the throat.

— 109 *The Vedant.*—A metaphyfical treatife on the nature of
God, which teacheth that matter is a mere delufion,
the fuppofed author of which is *Vyas*.

— 110 *Koothafta, or he who ftandeth on the pinnacle.*—The
divine effence, which, according to the opinion or
fome of their philofophers, is without quality, and
fitteth aloof inactive.

— 111 *There is another Pooroofh, &c. &c.*—This, and the following period, are fo full of myftery, that the Trans-
lator defpairs of revealing it to the fatisfaction of the
reader. Perhaps *Kreefhna* only means to collect into
one view the feveral appellations *Koothafta, Pooroofh,
Paramatma, Eefwar,* and *Pooroofhottama,* by which
the Deity is defcribed by as many different theologifts,
in order to expofe their various opinions refpecting
his nature, and unite them in one.

82 112 *Saftra.*—Any book of Divine authority.

86 113 *Zeal,* in the vulgar acceptation of the word, fignifies
the voluntary infliction of pain, the modes of doing
which, as practifed to this day by the zealots of India,

dia, are as various as they are horrible and aftonifhing. *Kreefhna*, by pointing out what true zeal is, tacitly condemns thofe extravagant mortifications of the flefh.

89   ¹¹⁴   *The Bards conceive, &c.*—The meaning of this period is too evident to require a note. But, in order to fhew that the commentators of India are not lefs fond of fearching for myftery, and wandering from the fimple path of their author into a labyrinth of fcholaftic jargon, than fome of thofe of more enlightened nations, who for ages have been labouring to entangle the plain unerring clew of our holy religion, the Tranflator, in this place, will intrude the following literal verfion of the comment written upon it by one *Sree-dhar Swamee*, whofe notes upon the whole are held in as much efteem as the text, which at this day, they fay, is unintelligible without them. It can feldom happen that a commentator is infpired with the fame train of thought and arrangement of ideas as the author whofe fentiments he prefumes to expound, efpecially in metaphyfical works. The Tranflator hath feen a comment, by a zealous Perfian, upon the wanton odes of their favorite Poet Hafiz, wherein every obfcene allufion is fublimated into a divine myftery, and the hoft and the tavern are as ingenioufly metamorphofed into their Prophet and his holy temple.

NOTE BY *SREE-DHAR SWAMEE*,
TO THE PASSAGE ABOVE ALLUDED TO.

" *The Bards, &c.*—The *Veds* fay—" Let him who
" longeth for children make offerings. Let him who
" longeth for heaven make offerings, &c. &c." The
" Bards underftand *Sannyas* to be a forfaking, that
" is, a total abandonment, of fuch works as are per-
" formed for the accomplifhment of a wifh, fuch
" works as are bound with the cord of defire. The
" *Pandeets* know, that is, they underftand, *Sannyas*
" to imply alfo a forfaking of all works, together
                                      " with

" with all their fruits. The difquifitors, that is, fuch
" as expound or make clear, call *Tyag* a forfaking of
" the fruit only of every work that is defirable,
" whether fuch as are ordained to be performed con-
" ftantly, or only at ftated periods; and not a for-
" faking of the work itself. But how can there be
" a forfaking of the fruit of fuch conftant and ftated
" works as have no particular fruit or reward annexed
" to them? The forfaking of a barren woman's
" child cannot be conceived.—It is faid—" Although
" one who longeth for heaven, or for a ftore of cat-
" tle, &c. fhould all his life perform the ceremonies
" which are called *Sandya*, or feed the fire upon the
" altar, and in thefe and the like ceremonies, no
" particular reward has ever been heard of; yet
" whilft the law is unable to engage a provident and
" wary man in a work where no human advantage
" is to be feen, at the fame time it ordaineth that
" even he who hath conquered the univerfe, &c.
" fhall perform facrifices; ftill for thefe, and the like
" religious duties, it hath appointed fome general re-
" ward."—But it is the opinion of *Gooroo*, that the
" law intended thefe works merely for its own ac-
" complifhment. Such a tenet is unworthy of notice,
" becaufe of the difficulty of obliging men to pay
" attention to thofe works.—It is alfo faid, that there
" is a reward annexed to the general and particular
" duties; that they who perform them fhall become
" inhabitants of the *Poonya-lok*; that by works the
" *Peetree-lok* is to be attained; that by good works
" crimes are done away, &c. &c. Wherefore it is
" properly faid,—that *they call Tyag a forfaking of the*
" *fruits of every aëtion.*"

90   115   *Five agents, &c.*—The five agents here implied, are
probably the foul, as fupervifor; the mind, as aëtor
or direëtor; the organs, as implements, &c.

—   116   *Nor is he bound thereby.*—He is not confined to mortal
birth.

—   117   *Gnan, Gneya, and Pareegnata.*—Wifdom, the objeët of
wifdom, and the fuperintending fpirit.

93   118   *Brahman*

F I N I S.

Breinigsville, PA USA
18 January 2011
253577BV00003B/51/P